MW00674857

THE UNRESOLVED DISPUTE

GILBERT COLEMAN, JR.

THE UNRESOLVED DISPUTE
Copyright © 2005 by Gilbert Coleman, Jr.

Unless otherwise noted, all Scripture quotations
are from the *Holy Bible, New King James Version.*
Copyright 1982 by Thomas Nelson, Inc.,
Nashville, TN. Used by permission.

Scripture quotations marked KJV are from
the *Holy Bible, King James Version.*

Scripture quotations marked NIV are from the
Holy Bible, New International Version. Copyright
© 1973, 1978, 1984, International Bible Society.
Used by Permission.

All rights reserved. No part of this publication
may be reproduced, stored in a retrieval system, or
transmitted in any form by means electronic, mechanical,
photocopying, recording or otherwise, except for the
inclusion of brief quotations in a review, without prior
permission in writing from the publisher.

ISBN: 0-9755311-7-4

Published by

LIFEBRIDGE
BOOKS
P.O. BOX 49428
CHARLOTTE, NC 28277

Printed in the United States of America.

DEDICATION

*This book is dedicated to my Lord and Savior
Jesus Christ who saved me and empowered me
with the gift to make all this possible.*

*I also want to thank God for my beloved wife
Debi, to whom I am very happily married, for
her love, support and dedication that allows me
to be free to minister to God's people. I can never
forget my children, Rashiid, Shelia, Nina, Darius and
Jahleel, as well as my grandchildren, Little Rashiid,
Julian, Majesty, Caleb and Kyla, who are a constant
source of love, encouragement and inspiration.*

*Last but not least, I want to dedicate this
book to my mother, Jessie Coleman, for being
used of God to bring me into the world, as well
as my late father, Gilbert Coleman, Sr. We thank God
for his memory and for the memory of my deceased
sisters, Willie Mae and Diane. Without all of
you I wouldn't be who I am today.*

ACKNOWLEDGMENTS

I am grateful to God for so many people, because with any project there are numerous individuals who help make it happen. In particular I thank God for David Molapo and his dear wife, Mamikie, for believing in me.

To Dr. Myles Munroe for inspiring me to write this book. Even though he may not know it, Bishop T.D. Jakes also had a hand in this because of a twenty minute conversation we had in Philadelphia that brought clarity to many things for me.

Thank you, Dr. Lucille Richardson, for your editing skills, even through great personal adversity. Suzette (Salmon): thank you for all your long hours of typing. To my son, Rashiid: you also gave much of your time and effort placing phone calls, sending emails, making copies and just overall being there whenever I needed you.

Last, I want to say "Thank you" to all of the Freedom Christian Bible Fellowship family for praying for me and for receiving the Word of the Lord which is helping all of us grow and fulfill the mandate of God for our ministry.

CONTENTS

FOREWORD

One of the greatest challenges of the 21st Century is the preservation and sanctity of marriage. Never before in history has marriage and family been under so much stress. During the past Century, the fight for equality between the male and female gender has taken conflict to another level. The declaration of the female's right to participate in social, political and economic processes in societies throughout the world have created a new equation for the value of the sexes in our post-modern society.

The historical biblical record of the creation of the male and female and the divine relationship structure between them as seen in the Holy Scripture is clear. Yet nowhere has there been more controversy over this issue than in the religious world. Churches, mosques and synagogues have been the battleground for marital conflict and many are still not sure whether the war will ever be over. However, it is important in addressing any issues to remember that no one knows the product like the manufacturer. Therefore, when there is confusion about the functioning of a product, we should refer to the manufacturer's manual—the Word of God.

In this book, *THE UNRESOLVED DISPUTE,* Gilbert Coleman, Jr., takes the reader back to the foundation of the relationship between male and female, and with his simple profound style, leaps over complicated theological boundaries and opens Scriptures to reveal the principles of marriage and relationships. He skillfully dissects the dynamic responsibilities, differences and uniqueness of the male and female and demonstrates how they compliment each other. His candid approach to the subject as a man, husband, father and pastor, releases wisdom from whose own experiences show exactly what men and women need to overcome the confusing alternatives of culture and social pressure.

I believe this book will become a classic and should be read by all who want to improve their relationships. I challenge you to dive into these pages and let the power of truth and practical principles transform your concept and attitude toward marriage relationships and life. This work brings the prospects of a happy marriage and healthy relationships from the shadow of fear and gives it a noble place in the light of God's original plan for mankind.

Read on and discover the hidden power of preparation for a successful marriage.

– Dr. Myles Munroe
Nassau, Bahamas

PREFACE

The casual observer would have to conclude that marriage as we have come to know it is in serious jeopardy of being redefined.

It is a sad day in any nation when the sanctity of marriage has to be protected by a Congressional order. This only reflects the temperament of a nation that has decided to push God out of the way and now seeks to live life as it chooses, regardless of what the spiritual implications may be. Of course, this is a repetition of the sentiment of previous generations, only now it is more blatant.

Divorce in America now stands at 51%. What a tragedy that more than half of the marriages initiated in this country fall apart. This should be an alarming statistic to all of us, however, the majority of the citizens of our nation seem to be quite content to live with this fact.

What precedent are we setting for our children? The message we are presently sending is that it's okay to co-habitate—meaning there is absolutely nothing wrong with relationships which carry no accountability or responsibility. What is even more alarming is that of the 51% marriage failure statistic, the divorce rate in the church is higher than that of the secular world.

Think of it! We have the Word of God and His Holy Spirit dwelling on the inside and still cannot manage to maintain strong and stable marriages. Could it be we have decided to join the world in their quest to be rid of God's sovereign rule over us? Something has to change.

I am persuaded it is high time those of us who *care* begin to stand up and speak out against the weakening of spiritual and moral values in our nation and around the world. This is no time to be nonchalant or silent concerning the issues that stand before us, threatening to totally erode the very fibre and core of our society—marriage and the family.

All too often I have counseled couples who finally reach the place where they believe the only resolution to their problem is divorce. Both parties say, "There is nothing left to hold on to." They would much rather just go their separate ways.

What these people are actually saying is they no longer want to *work* at their marriage. To me it implies that from the beginning they probably didn't have a good understanding of what it takes to make a marriage work.

Two people must be committed to the union; not just to the person they marry. There is a vast difference in the two concepts. When two individuals are only committed to a person, failure is imminent. I say that because of how we as human beings vacillate from one thing to another. Consequently, we do not always present a picture of stability.

However, for the people who are committed to the *marriage* their vow is to the covenant they made, therefore, they are not looking for a way of escape every time adversity rears its ugly head.

By virtue of our humanness, trials and tribulations are going to surface, but a husband and wife must learn to navigate stormy seas together. The world's people—and particularly the body of Christ—must resolve that marriage is worth saving.

If we are going to see our children and grandchildren grow up in a healthy familial environment, the time to act is now. It all starts with allowing Christ to become the "Head" of all our life. When that takes place, the only choice we will make is a "God choice."

– Gilbert Coleman, Jr.

INTRODUCTION

In the beginning, the need for fellowship was a vital part of God's creation plan for man, for God said:

"It is not good for the man to be alone.
I will make a helper suitable for him."
−GENESIS 2:18

Our Creator is a God of order, and He has purposed that every living creature come together to foster proper relationships in society. His intent is to guarantee the full expression of Himself. So to make a helper signifies man's *strength*—for all he was called to be and do was inadequate in itself. God knew exactly what man needed to complement him in accomplishing his daily work and procreation.

Just as there are legislative laws which regulate our lifestyles and promote harmony (instead of breeding chaos and dissension), God also has instituted rules and regulations to steer our relationships into a harmonious wholeness. He does not desire to restrict our freedom or capacity to enjoy each other. Instead, He wishes that we enjoy life to the fullest capacity, but only according to biblical principles.

God's design is for people to enjoy fellowship with

one another. We need relationships and it is God's will that we live in harmony, *"endeavoring to keep the unity of the Spirit in the bond of peace"* (Ephesians 4:3 NKJV).

To be in harmony means we will *"be of the same mind toward one another"* (Romans 12:16 KJV). We must be *"be like-minded toward one another, according to Christ Jesus"* (Romans 15:5 NKJV).

While we may have different opinions concerning certain things, it is Christ who unites us less we enter into unresolved disputes in our personal lives. Thus, the lingering issues carry over into other relationships with our family, friends, co-workers, society and marriage, because—as we will discover—they were never resolved between the first two people at the beginning of creation.

CHAPTER ONE

LIFE IN THE GARDEN

And they heard the sound of the Lord
God walking in the garden in the cool of the day:
and Adam and his wife hid themselves from the
presence of the Lord God among the trees of the
garden. And the Lord God called to Adam and said
to him, Where are You? So he said, I heard your voice
in the garden, and I was afraid because I was naked;
and hid myself. And He said, Who told you that
you were naked? Have you eaten from the tree of
which I commanded you that you should not eat?
Then the man said, The woman whom You gave to
be with me, she gave me of the tree, and I ate.

And the Lord God said to the woman, What
is this you have done? The woman said,
The serpent deceived me, and I ate.
– GENESIS 3:8-13 K J V

Then the Lord God said, Behold, the man has
become like one of Us, to know good and evil.

17

*And now lest he put out his hand and take also of
the tree of life, and eat, and live forever—therefore
the Lord God sent him out of the garden of Eden to till
the ground from which he was taken. So He drove out
the man; and He placed cherubim at the east of the
garden of Eden, and a flaming sword which turned
every way, to guard the way to the tree of life*

— VERSES 22-24

The series of events which took place in the "Garden
of Eden" set the stage for what we see today in
relationships between husbands and wives. The Bible
tells us that the Lord came down to talk with Adam and
Eve because of their disobedience and intent to be
independent of Him.

The first thing God said to Adam was, *"Adam, where
are you?"*

God was not referring to his geographical location.
He wanted to know where Adam stood with *Him* in his
personal relationship, because the word "eden" means
"pleasure," or "delight." It represented a complete state
or environment of unbroken communion between God
and man.

"WHERE DO WE STAND?"

When we transgress God's law, the first thing He's
going to do is question our position in Him. The
Almighty wants to know, "Where is your relationship
with Me? I understand that you have your own free will,

but you have violated My law, now where are we, where do we stand? Do we still have the same intimacy?"

Let's look at ourselves, rather than Adam. Because we break God's law, the question becomes, "Why did we do it?" Far too often the answer is that our actions were performed knowingly—and in many instances our behavior is premeditated. We knew exactly what we were doing when we took the action.

So, God asks, "Where are you? What is our relationship now that you have committed this act?"

Adam said, *"I heard your voice in the garden...and I was afraid."* As soon as God questioned Adam, he became fearful.

What happens when we mess up? Usually, the first thing we do is run and hide.

We don't pray or read the Bible, because we allow the spirit of guilt and condemnation to come upon us. Then we allow our sin to *control* us and we stop talking to God.

NAKED, STRIPPED!

Never forget that the Lord desires to communicate with His children. He wants us to reason together and solve the problem because there's no need to remain in such a state. It needs to be resolved. That's what the Father is longing for.

However, rather than wanting to repair our fellowship with God, we panic and run because we are afraid. Why? Because we are naked, stripped! We've been exposed, and we don't like the consequences.

As soon as God removes the covers, who we truly are comes to the forefront—and often it is not a pretty picture. We don't like being laid bare, especially to other people. The Bible says "open rebuke is better than secret love," but we still don't like to be chastised publicly. The Bible also declares:

Rebuke them openly, so that others may also fear.
– 1 TIMOTHY 5:20

God wants us to have a reverential fear and respect for Him. This means we must correct people openly, so others will be aware. Since individuals do not want to be exposed, they will change their behavior.

So Adam said, *"I was naked."* And, *"I hid myself"* (Genesis 3:10).

God asked, *"Who told you that you were naked?"* (v.11). There was no way Adam and Eve could see themselves as being disrobed, because prior to that time, they were both clothed with the glory of God.

The first man and woman had a special intimacy; and now they were hiding from God and each other. Before this moment they weren't walking around with their hands covering their nakedness. Now that they've eaten from the tree, rather than seeing one another as being beautiful, they viewed each other as dirty, and began covering themselves.

REALITIES OF LIFE

Often, husbands and wives act the same way. "Turn the light out!" they say, not wanting their nakedness to be seen. Many openly confess they do not like being exposed.

Some retreat inside themselves for a lifetime, because they believe their bodies are filthy and should not be seen by others.

This is what they have been taught, and such a viewpoint becomes imbedded in their thought process. There are those who have been abused, and see themselves as corrupted and vile. Sadly, these issues are realities of life.

In Genesis 3:10, Adam said, *"I hid myself." And God asked him "Who told you that you were naked, did you eat of the tree that I commanded you not to eat of?"* (v.11).

God reminded Adam of what He said. When the Lord

21

renders judgment, it is against something He told man *not* to do. Then He reminds us of it, so we can't say He is unfair.

Next, Adam reasoned, *"The woman whom You gave to be with me, she gave me of the tree, and I ate"* (v.12).

"ADAM, YOU NEED A WIFE"

The man was given the ultimate responsibility, yet he quicky passed the buck: "Lord, it's not me, it's her! In fact, God, if you had not given her to me, I wouldn't be in this situation. After all, I was down here tending the garden, minding my own business, and one day you came along and said, 'Adam, you need a wife.'"

As scripture records, Adam said, *"I ate"* (v.12).

After addressing the man first, God then addressed the woman: *"And the Lord God said unto the woman, What is this...that you have done?"* (v.13).

The Creator was still dealing with them individually. Having dealt with Adam's action, He addressed Eve's behavior, by saying, *"Now what did you do?"* The woman replied, *"The serpent beguiled me, he tricked me, and deceived me and I did eat"* (v. 13).

OUT OF ORDER

The question is: how did she become deceived? Eve knew the law since she had an open conversation with the devil. But the woman thought that in some way she didn't have everything Adam possessed, because the

Bible records, "She saw the tree as something to make one wise" (v. 6). Eve was already wise, yet she failed to realize it. So she allowed Satan to trick her into thinking she was not equal to her husband, even though God had blessed them and said, *"...be fruitful and multiply, and have dominion over the earth"* (Genesis 1:28).

Eve already had a "dominion spirit" within her, though she felt she didn't have what her husband possessed. When I say *dominion spirit,* I don't mean domineering. I am simply referring to Eve's God-given ability to dominate everything in the earth. So she had to show herself as equal to him. Eve said the devil tricked her, but she never blamed her husband! Although Adam was supposed to be her protector and covering, she never accused him of being out of order.

Some women like to shield their men even when they know their spouse is completely in the wrong. Many will even lie for a man because they don't want the world to know the weaknesses of their partner. This protective spirit women have towards men started with Eve and continues even today.

"RED CLAY"

The Bible records Adam was made from the dust of the ground. *"There was no rain in those days, because there was no man to till the ground."* (Genesis 2:5). In other words, there was no man to take care of the garden.

What happened? God did not send rain, instead there was a mist that came up from the ground to water the vegetation on the entire planet. He sent the moisture to make the clay, because Adam's name means *"red clay."* So in order to get the necessary substance to work with, God had to supply water in order to shape Adam's body. The Hebrew word for "mist" actually means, "to make a canopy as in a Jewish wedding." It is the same word for "worship."

Not only did Adam and Eve violate God's law, but God put within the clay the ability to worship and marry. Their behavior, however, delayed the marriage; and they were not giving the kind of worship that should have come forth, because their worship was in dirt.

The ability to worship has always been within our being, but we need the tree of life to activate it.

Adam had the ability to worship God instinctively, but he refused. We also have the same power, yet we often deny it.

Our capability for worship has always been within our being, but we need the tree of life to make it come alive. As a result, our relationships are not always the way they should be, because we do not worship as God intends. Often, men and women come together with the Spirit of God dwelling inside them, and are still not able to praise and worship.

THORNS AND THISTLES

So God cursed Adam and told him to work, and live by the sweat of his brow.

*Therefore the Lord God sent him out of the Garden
of Eden to till the ground from which he was taken. So
He drove out the man; and He placed cherubim at the east
of the garden of Eden, and a flaming sword which turned
every way, to guard the way to the tree of life.*
– GENESIS 3:23-24

The ground was blessed prior to this event and then the earth was cursed. This is why life is so hard for us, because God put a curse on the land. He said, *"It's going to bring forth thorns and thistles"* (Genesis 3:18).

The reason a snake crawls on its belly today is because it was cursed. Those who study such things tell us in the beginning of creation the snake used to stand on its haunches. Every time you see a snake slithering, remember this is due to its part in the fall of man.

Then God resolved what He had to do. He also cursed the woman by stating she would bring forth children in pain, labor and sorrow (verse 16). The Lord settled the matter with man and woman, but the issue which existed *between* Adam and Eve was never resolved.

Can you imagine how Eve felt when they were standing before Almighty God, especially when Adam told God it was her fault (verse 12)? She was human, so she harbored thoughts of her husband "betraying" her to God.

Adam also had the same negative emotions when they left the presence of the Creator with an unresolved dispute. He had to live with the thought that he disappointed God, but couldn't bring himself to accept the blame for the disappointment.

CHAPTER TWO

OUTSIDE THE GARDEN

No other form of earthly life plays a more vital role than mankind. In essence, the world stands or falls based on the actions of individuals.

The sin of one man, Adam, corrupted the world, yet God desires to reveal His truth and beauty through redeemed mankind. The curse of man's disobedience was reinforced by the expulsion of Adam and Eve from "the Garden" (Genesis 3:23), the place of their unique communion with God.

Genesis 4:1 says, *"And Adam knew Eve his wife."* To say they knew each other expresses the close sexual experience of marriage. The Scripture also states, *"and she conceived and bore Cain...and Abel"* (v.2).

Their children were both born outside the Garden of Eden. This means Cain and Abel were not under the protective shield of God, because they were born under the covering of a dispute.

*From that one act of disobedience with Adam,
sin has been transferred to the whole world.*

This curse has passed from generation to generation, and is the reason we have conflict in our homes and relationships today. The Bible says:

> *Therefore, just as through one man sin entered
> the world, and death through sin, and thus death
> spread to all men, because all sinned.*
> —ROMANS 5:12

Because we are sinful in nature—born in sin, and shaped in iniquity—we all have transgression within our own soul. This being the case, there is no doubt we all *have* sinned, *are* sinning and *will* sin.

DO WE UNDERSTAND?

A man and woman's relationship can be very difficult due to a lack of understanding, low tolerance and an absence of respect. We simply do not comprehend each other's roles, uniqueness, differences, and varying needs.

This deficiency of understanding is the reason we have such disparity between males and females. It not only affects husbands and wives, but also men and women trying to relate to each other. As a result, it becomes difficult attempting to resolve issues if we don't take the time to understand each other.

Once we realize God made us, we will have a deeper

respect for humanity and a greater appreciation for others.

Often, we can't truly value our mate because we want them to be like us. Many Christians have varying levels of spiritual maturity, and because we don't operate on the same level, there is a great void in our relationships. Some have renewed minds and are walking fully clothed in righteousness. Others say they have matured in the Lord, yet show low tolerance, no patience, and don't allow people room to grow.

The "real deal" is: you're not where you think you are. If you really were, then the fruit called "patience" would be preeminent in your life. This low tolerance can cause us to see our bond with others as being a burden, rather than a blessing—which leads to a lack of respect for our mate.

There is a need for the restoration of understanding, tolerance, love and respect since we don't have the agape love we should possess.

Since there was never true reconciliation between Adam and Eve, they transferred these burdens to us. Therefore, what must take place today is our desire to be reconciled.

Sometimes we can't even speak to one another with civility since we are so intolerant of our individual differences. Our home is supposed to be a place of celebration, not mere toleration.

Far too often we try to settle racial differences in the world, but the greater reconciliation must be between man and woman. We need to sit down with each other and openly discuss the matters we know are deep issues of concern. We can't continue *thinking* things are going to get better without mutual cooperation.

"NO MATTER WHAT!"

Some feel if they pray and fast, sooner or later everything will be just fine. But, that's not how it works! Here's the problem. We enter into a relationship with the knowledge there are deficiencies in the other person's life. We knew, before we ever said "I do," that the individual had some unresolved issues. However, we stood at the altar and declared we were going to accept our spouse "for better or worse."

When we utter those words, "I do," we're saying, "I do" to who they are and who they will become. "That's how much we love each other." The Bible says:

> *Therefore, if anyone is in Christ, he is*
> *a new creation; old things have passed away;*
> *behold, all things have become new.*
> – 2 CORINTHIANS 5:17

This includes your attitude, because everything now has a new beginning.

All this is from God, who reconciled us to himself through Christ and gave us the ministry of reconciliation.
– 2 CORINTHIANS 5:18 NIV

This message resides *inside* you. How? Through Jesus Christ who reconciled the world to Himself, not imputing our trespasses. The Bible says, not only do you have the message, but also you have the specific word. God declares you have "in you" whatever is needed to reconcile with your spouse, friend or family. Therefore, we cannot say we don't have the ability to accomplish the task.

Perhaps inwardly we don't want to make things right, because we would rather remain angry, stressed, under pressure, etc., as opposed to being conciliatory, saying, "We need to work this out. Come, let's reason together."

LAYING BLAME

Obviously, there had to be some marital problems between Adam and Eve when they were expelled from Eden because they both received knowledge of good and evil. The ability to scheme, connive, and undermine existed because these traits came from the spirit of evil which now inhabited them. Adam and Eve's minds were no longer totally in tune with God, and they had the ability to entertain all influences and suggestions of the devil.

Imagine how they must have reacted being relegated to the wilderness and having to physically toil. Adam likely looked at this woman and lamented, "If it hadn't

31

been for you, I wouldn't have to work like this!"

We don't know how long Eve lived, but Adam survived 900 years—and he probably re-lived those thoughts every day.

There were also problems passed on to their children, because Cain and Abel were born outside the Garden of Eden.

*And Adam lived one hundred and
thirty years, and begot a son in his own likeness
after his image, and named him Seth.*
— GENESIS 5:3

The word "Seth" means substitute. He was a replacement for Abel who was killed by Cain. Therefore, the first two individuals born after the fall had evil in them. Cain came against his own brother, killed him in the wilderness, and God reminded Adam that they were created in his likeness.

THE POISONED TREE

We must conquer the Tree of the Knowledge of Good and Evil if we desire to have balanced male-female relationships. There were two trees in the garden; one represented life, the other death.

God told Adam and Eve to stay away from death because He knew it was poison. The Creator said, *"In the day that you eat of it, you shall surely die"* (Genesis 1:17). He was talking about a spiritual separation, not a physical death, although eventually it would come. Initially God wanted man to live eternally only with the knowledge of good. He would *tell* man what was evil. That's how it was intended, but it never reached that point.

The Tree of the Knowledge of Good and Evil not only affected Adam and Eve, it affects us. Until a man and a woman make a conscious decision they are going to let go of this "Tree," there will always be disparity and conflict within our homes.

We must desire to accept the *newness* God proclaims is ours. Although the Lord says it belongs to us, everyone does not receive it.

DISAPPOINTMENT

Much turmoil exists in families because both parties are disappointed, sometimes highly so:

- The woman is disappointed because the man will not lead, and the man is disappointed because the woman will not follow.
- The woman is disappointed because the man will not meet her needs, and the man is disappointed because the woman will not respect him.
- The woman is disappointed because the man will not pay any attention to her, while the man is disappointed because the woman does not appreciate him.

Since she doesn't celebrate him and he doesn't

meet her needs, their dashed hopes lead to frustration, which eventually results in emotional detachment.

Our home should be a place of celebration, and not a place of toleration.

Much anguish and conflict exists because the two people really are not united together even though they live in the same house.

Often we hear "I'm living with this person, but I'm still lonely. I have this longing within me. I want to be satisfied. I want to be fulfilled, yet I can't find happiness with the person to whom I said, 'I do.' I guess I'm stuck here for the rest of my life until he (or she) dies."

It's a sad and frightening thought, but true.

THE BATTLE FOR POWER

It is not until both man and woman are in pursuit of the Tree of Life that the battle for power will cease. This is another major struggle in our household.

Husbands and wives are at odds with one another because the question has never been settled as to who will be in control. We wonder, "Who's in charge?" Can we ever finally come to the place where we truly resolve who is supposed to be the leader in the home?

In many relationships, especially in marriage, we are overly concerned about feelings: how we are going to be addressed; how we are going to be taken care of; what kind of attention will we receive; what kind of affection.

The question seems to be one sided. It's all, "What about me? What about me?"

The greatest person in far too many lives is "Me, myself and I." Yet, we are supposed to be in the union because we desire to help meet the needs of the other person. What happened to expressing agape love, which says that we should desire giving, though we don't always receive?

We should be in pursuit of the Tree of Life, which is representative of Christ. As soon as we have Jesus centered and anchored in our being, there is no doubt we will enter a place of worship—worship as God intended.

OUT OF ORDER?

Many men and women spend much of their time, trying to prove to one another they can make it by themselves. Some women rationalize, "I'm strong, powerful, knowledgeable, gifted, talented and I have my own abilities. So guess what? I really don't need you!"

Sadly, two people are often in the same household feeling they don't need each other. The problem is they are convinced they can take care of themselves as they did before they met their spouse. As a result, they have not joined as "one," realizing they complete each other.

The woman's attitude may be: "I can make it without you. No problem! I was working when I met you. I will keep on working and make my own money. I owned my house and car when we met, and I know how to provide for myself."

This is out of order! A woman should not be

attempting to prove to the man how independent she can be. The bottom line is, now that Christ is in her life, she's supposed to be at the place where she becomes fulfilled while sustained; independent while submissive.

In the process she doesn't lose her individuality, because God is not telling her to become a robot. Rather, He wants to make sure the image of Christ is in their home. Therefore, as a man submits to Christ, a woman submits to Him through her husband.

It's not about a wife thinking she can make it alone. No man wants a woman who is as tough as he is. We must understand that within the bonds of marriage, a husband must be able to become as masculine as he's supposed to be in the union, and the woman should become as feminine as she's supposed to be in the same relationship. There should be a constant, equal exchange between a husband and wife. Together, they achieve their full potential.

If a husband and wife will commit to commonly share, then no one is searching for power or control, because the Holy Spirit will control him or her.

You may conclude you can have a better life without your spouse, but according to the Word:

Nevertheless, neither is man independent of woman, nor woman independent of man in the Lord.

For as woman came from man, even so man also comes through woman; but all things are from God.
– 1 CORINTHIANS 11:12

Too much time is wasted jockeying for *position* in the household, yet there's no need for either party to be battling for *anything*. Some think they're going to be pushed aside, or will no longer have credibility or visibility. However, from God's perspective we have a specific role to fulfill and we must complete it.

HOME COMES FIRST

Today's society is structured so that women are much more career-oriented than in the past. Due to the present economic pressures, women have been forced to seek employment outside the home to help sustain the family. As a result they struggle to juggle work, household needs and the raising of children. Unfortunately, many youngsters are left alone.

Parents are still responsible for being keepers of their home. The Bible refers to the word "keeper" as guardian. Therefore women must be accountable to their household first and to their career second. Likewise, men must be responsible for sustaining their entire household, even if it includes a working wife.

LEARNING TO LEAN

God expects a man to be the foundation of his home. This means his wife should be able to stand in front of him with the children in front of both of them. This is so she may always lean back on him (Remember the woman

37

came out of the man), and the children in turn lean back on them.

God devised this plan. However many would much rather listen to what society preaches, and as a result they have no foundation.

Some men have been pushed away from their position as the head of the family. They are disappointed with their dysfunctional role and as a result, they'd rather go where they can be celebrated. They fall back to the Adam excuse: *"This woman you gave me..."* Eventually they stop bringing their emotions home and some end up committing adultery.

"OF ONE MIND"

We have expended so much energy into the world system that when we walk through the font door at home there is very little conversation. Often, the woman desires to talk while the man would much rather bury his head in a newspaper, not wanting to listen or be attentive to her needs. When she wants to lean on him, she can't, because she realizes if she does she is going to fall—and there is no one there to catch her!

In 1 Peter 3:8-12, we are reminded of all the other steps a husband and wife ought to take for each other. He says, "we must be of one mind, having compassion one for another, love as brethren. Be pitiful, courteous, not rendering evil for evil."

To put it bluntly, we should show consideration for each other's feelings and not act spitefully or selfishly. Because your spouse lashes out, saying something derogatory doesn't mean you should respond in like manner. Peter says, "Or railing for railing," which means "accusation for accusation." If a person accuses you of something, it doesn't mean you've got to try and find fault against them.

Peter also adds that rather than trying to find evil things to speak, we should choose good to say to them—and *about* them. By applauding and celebrating each other we can inherit a blessing.

According to 1 Peter 3:7, our prayers will be hindered if we are not of one accord with our mate. This is not only for men, but women as well. Many women feel it's not worth the effort because they're exhausted and frustrated. They just can't hang on any longer.

The Bible says:

> *Be not weary in well doing, for in due*
> *season we shall reap if we faint not.*
> – GALATIANS 6:9

There can be no harvest unless you do some sowing. This means you must begin to seed your love, attention, effort, and affection. As you sow these attributes, you will also reap them.

It's time to come to the place where you're planting what you desire to harvest. Plus, it is essential we return to the position God established for men and women. There is a specific assignment He has planned.

KNOW YOUR ROLE
A man's role is to lead, protect and provide. There are

men who will not step up to the plate and do what is required spiritually to make sure their home is always safe and intact. They must provide leadership and guidance for the direction God is saying a wife and the children are supposed to be headed. This is the man's role.

Here's one of the reasons some men won't lead. We say this jokingly, but it's true. You're faced with a decision you know you need to make, but what you say instead is "Let me talk to the boss first."

Please understand ladies, I am not trying to imply a woman has no input in what needs to be done in the home, because the Bible says there should be *agreement*. However, it does not mean your husband has to come to you and ask permission.

Most women understand that if they are not in agreement, all they have to do is show a certain attitude. They are well aware the effect their demeanor has on their man. When this is displayed, he may even change his mind concerning something he knows God told him to do.

THE ISSUE OF SUBMISSION

Women must understand the power and influence they have over a man and not abuse it. Some women do not permit their spouse to step forward because they have it in their mind to lead. When you marry, however, you are saying he is the one who is fulfilling what it is you desire in this life. He makes you complete, and is therefore qualified to lead the home—and you must be willing to follow his lead.

When you said, "I do," that's exactly what you agreed to. Remember, marriage is a covenant.

Therefore, just as the church is subject to Christ,
so let the wives be to their own husbands in everything.
—EPHESIANS 5:24

God said wives are to submit to their husbands in *everything*. That does not imply they don't have any say. It simply means someone has to make the final decision—and God said it should be the man.

Women who resist letting go of the reins is one of the reasons we have a battle for power and control. God specifically says the man will lead because he is the head of the woman. Man must protect, provide and lead.

The woman's role then is to respond, nurture and provide moral influence in society. Women, please observe how vital your role is. You shape our future generations. Your assignment includes making your man feel he's the only man on earth. You were created to be a "responder" to his leadership.

When a woman responds to her husband's
leadership, she responds to his love.

A man can go out of his way and make the effort to do certain things for a woman, yet she doesn't react properly. He can buy her favorite flowers and she thanks him with a little peck on the cheek, then quickly throws the bouquet in a vase and goes back to her daily routine. Upset, he responds, "Is that all? Come on. I took the time to think about you today. I bought you flowers. Is this the thanks I get?"

How are you making him feel special? He lovingly thought of you, expressing his feelings with flowers, a gift or a card. Where is the joy which demonstrates receiving and giving?

Sometimes you've got to be willing to give, even though you may not necessarily be a recipient of anything in return. Again, you must understand your role. The problem is: too many women are not comfortable with their assignment and feel in some way or another they have been taken advantage of.

A "HELPER"

You must fulfill your God-given purpose, which means you are to take care of the mission the Lord has given to you. If you put God first, He will delight in presenting you with the desires of your heart.

Women must not view their "helper" role as being subservient. You're not a slave—neither are you a doormat. Nobody is going to walk over you because of your assigned role. Even Jesus came as a true servant and promised to send us the Holy Spirit as our "Helper". The word used for Holy Spirit is *"Paraclete"* which also means "helper." As the psalmist prays:

But I am poor and needy; Make haste to me, oh God! You are my help and my deliverer; oh Lord, do not delay.
—PSALM 70:5

In Genesis, the word "woman" and "helper" are the same. So if God refers to Himself as a helper, then women are to be honored for being assigned the same role.

Here's another example. If one mate is uncomfortable with his or her position, it will subsequently cause the other partner to become uncomfortable as well. If a partner does not fulfill the expected duty, then the spouse will sense what's happening and become non-responsive.

FACING THE REAL ISSUES

Often couples do not truly spend time talking about serious issues. I'm referring to sensitive topics where you make a pointed statement to your mate which may even seem hurtful.

There are instances when you may need to communicate what you know is true, but still refrain from doing so because you're afraid of the response. As a result the subject stays buried and there is no opportunity for change.

Remember, God changes hearts, not you.

Let's face it. You married a mate with flaws! You also said you were willing to put up with it, "For better or for worse, for richer or poorer, in sickness and in health, till death do us part."

Though men and women desire comfort, companionship and fulfillment, their emotional needs are vastly different. A man does not always understand the needs of a woman. He may see her as being weak, too sensitive and out of control. However, her emotional temperature may be due to pressure that is mounting inside. Perhaps she is stressed out.

Because she is so filled with tension, she's prone to unpredictable outbursts. The man is desperately trying to understand, and all he can think to say is, "What's wrong with you? Why are you acting like this?"

Women need to be able to express their inner feelings and men need to let them talk and release what's in their hearts. It does not mean a man has no emotional needs, because he does. All he asks is for his wife to applaud him.

APPLAUSE! APPLAUSE!

A man will do certain things looking for at least one person to be his cheerleader. He wants to hear "That was great, I loved it!" If nobody else thought it was great, you should. If not one other person is there to celebrate him, you ought to compliment and encourage—making him feel good about himself.

There are certain women who are not concerned how their mate feels because he hasn't yet met all of her needs. So she thinks to herself, "When he responds to me the right way, maybe I'll reciprocate."

If you truly are in Christ, your mind should also be renewed. Remember, your role is to nurture.

Allow me to offer this word of advice: If you have a daughter, you should make sure she understands how to treat a man before she gets married.

Men, if you have a son, that young man ought to know the wealth and value of a woman before he becomes engaged. He must understand how to treat the woman as a treasured gift in his life—and it's your responsibility as a parent to teach him such things.

MATURITY AND GROWTH

Far too often we speak to our mate and tell them a particular truth about themselves they don't receive well. They feel we are insensitive to their needs when we are only trying to help. They misinterpret our motives and conclude we are patronizing, putting them down or trying to make them feel less than the person they really are.

In the meantime we are concerned with their maturity and growth, yet they don't like receiving our counsel. Though they do not immediately accept what is offered, we must not move away from what we know is going to help them develop.

Spiritually, we need to assist in building their life in the Lord. We are supposed to help bring God's Kingdom to earth, but the Kingdom must first come to us as individuals. Once that happens, it will touch the world.

RESOLVE THE ISSUES AT HOME

What happens in your home is what you bring to God's House. So if the airwaves are clogged, it is because our spiritual arteries are blocked with damaging debris which should have been removed. Instead we drag these things to church, and the next thing you know, the praise and worship leaders are trying hard, struggling, attempting to get "angry" people to praise the Lord.

These disgruntled spouses stand in church thinking, "I'm not with him," or "I'm not praising God with her." In some cases, even while they're standing in the congregation, their backs are turned to each other. Some even sit in different sections of the sanctuary.

There are also those who role-play—holding hands and pulling close together because they don't want anybody else to know what they're going through. They fake worship and try to pray with an impure heart. The psalmist writes:

> *Who shall ascend into the hill of the Lord,*
> *and who shall stand in His holy place? He that*
> *has clean hands and a pure heart.*
> —PSALM 24:3-4

Such problems should have been prayed over and dealt with before entering into the presence of the Lord.

> *Then we will no longer be infants tossed back*
> *and forth by the waves, and blown here and there*
> *by every wind of teaching, and by the cunning and*
> *craftiness of men in their deceitful scheming. Instead,*
> *speaking the truth in love, we will in all things grow*
> *up into Him who is the head, that is Christ.*
> —EPHESIANS 4:14-15 NIV

Whatever you say to your spouse should only be for the sake of maturity; to help your relationship become stronger, by providing more intimacy and depth of honesty.

Think about your marriage. How deep can it go? What can you say to your spouse that you feel he or she will receive? Can you talk about sensitive matters without becoming angry?

A key factor that's missing in the family is leadership, because we attempt to exchange male/female roles which only leads to confusion. Through biblical leadership, using Jesus as our model, we will learn that the wife can't be the husband, and the husband can't be the wife.

The man, in following the ultimate leader, pours into his wife what God has poured into him, and together they can resolve the issues in their home.

CHAPTER THREE

IMAGES AND EXPECTATIONS

There was once a young soldier who became blinded in war and was rehabilitated at an army hospital. During the course of his convalescence, he fell in love with one of the nurses who took great care of him, and they were later married. He had an amazing love for her and was totally devoted.

One day he overheard some guests in his home talking about him and his wife. "It was fortunate for her that he was blind, since he never would have married such a homely woman if he had eyes."

The sightless soldier entered the room and responded, "I heard what you said, and I thank God from the depths of my heart for my blindness which might have kept me from seeing the marvelous worth of the soul of this woman who is my wife. She is the most noble character I have ever known and I love her." Then he added, "If the outward appearance of her features may have masked her inward beauty, then I gained greatly by having lost my sight."

This story should remind us that God is far more concerned with the heart than with the outward appearance (1 Samuel 16:7). He prefers holiness above glamour (I Peter 3:4).

HOPES AND DREAMS

Nearly all marriages begin with high hopes and great expectations for the future. However, in the process we often form certain images in our mind which we desire to see in our spouse. Then, if for any reason our mates do not live up to that image, we tend to treat them according to what we pictured.

With such expectations, we draw the curtain of fantasy over the stage of reality. Often, the truth of who they are was already established before we exchanged vows, but because we were so much in love we excused things that undoubtedly were red flags. We pushed aside warnings and though the caution signals were constantly blinking, we chose to ignore them, and ran through all the red lights. You know what happens when we don't heed stop signs—eventually we're going to wind up in an accident.

People will create their own fantasy world where they pretend everything is okay. They believe miraculously their mate is going to become someone different. However, unless the Holy Spirit transforms the individual, what was from the beginning will be to the end.

AN IRREVOCABLE AGREEMENT

Webster defines happiness as "the satisfaction, or

realization of one's greatest desire." This is what everyone is searching for—and believe they are going to find in another human being.

One day you wake up living under the same roof with another individual you are totally displeased with. You're dejected because your mate is not making you happy. Yet, when you married, you were already aware of some of your spouse's shortcomings.

Marriage is a covenant, not a contract.

The word "marriage" is not a job description. It is not to be used as a weapon to threaten, "I can end the contract if you don't do what the paper says."

No. Marriage is a covenant rather than a legal contract. It is an irrevocable agreement which says a husband and wife care for each other so much until they're willing to accept their differences without demanding change.

There are certain desires in your life, which no human being can fulfill. Only God can provide *everything* you need. So, we must stop trying to put other people in "boxes." It only frustrates their lives and makes them unhappy when you can't find contentment in your own situation.

The reality of life is we must learn to give our mate the room to grow without forcing unfair demands upon him or her that are birthed from our own selfishness.

"FERVENT" LOVE

Let's take an honest inventory and look at ourselves. There are days we are contrary, mean, obstinate, uncaring, refuse to listen, and the last thing we want to do is help. We make unfair demands, which reflect our own self-centered desires.

Marriage is supposed to be a life of service—not demanding from your spouse and throwing temper tantrums when things don't go according to your plans. Scripture tells us:

> *...The end of all things is at hand; therefore be serious and watchful in your prayers.*
> *– 1 PETER 4:7-8*

If there are flaws and weaknesses in the other person's life, Peter says we must be on our face praying, investing our time as an intercessor for those we cherish.

He also tells us to have "fervent" love for one another. The word *fervent* means steadfast and consistent.

There should be no breach in how you love your partner. It must be continual—which means there should never be a lull in your love relationship. Our affection needs to be growing and intensifying, not diminishing or weakening. According to the words of Peter, we should not allow anything else to get in the way, for love will cover a multitude of sins.

No one should have to live daily under the watchful eye of his or her mate's scrutiny. Neither should anyone have to wake up wondering what his or her spouse is doing in secret.

Often what we interpret as a fault in our mate is nothing more than an exposure of our own insecurities.

We want to blame the other person for our personal unhappiness when we have issues that keep us insecure—especially when we know we are not in control of certain facets or elements of our life.

What happens at that point is we attempt to maintain control over the other person so the search light is taken off of us. We want to blame them for everything, when in truth we are the weak partner.

Some of us have baggage we have been holding onto for years. We have never been able to vanquish these things since we are unable to conquer ourselves.

FINGER-POINTING?

The reason some people get married is because they need another individual to solidify their life. However, the Bible tells us to stop shifting the blame:

> *Therefore you are inexcusable, O man, whoever you are who judge, for in whatever you judge another you condemn yourself; for you who judge practice the same thing.*
> — ROMANS 2:1

53

In effect, God is saying, "I'm not letting you off the hook, because you are just as bad as the other person. So stop pointing your finger."

The only reason we are readily able to identify a negative character trait is because we do the same things ourselves.

THE SUBMISSION FACTOR

In this, the 21st Century, a man must know God has called him to be the leader. In their ignorance, however, there are men who lead by suppressing the woman. This is also practiced in many occult religions where the husband will tell their wife that God wants them to be quiet, or make unrealistic demands.

However, society encourages women to be liberated and independent. Don't dare succumb to any man or listen to that type of talk about submission.

This initiates a power struggle because the woman wants to be free, as does the man. What's the result? In many cases, the man is determined to be a man, while the woman is determined to be a man too!

This battle is being fought in millions of households. It is an issue of power, authority and control. Sadly, the two people who are enduring this battle have not yet become comfortable with their God-given role. It also indicates they are not pleased with themselves, and have not grown up to be mature individuals reconciled to doing things God's way.

The household is not meant to be man-controlled, nor

woman-controlled; it is ordained to be Holy Spirit controlled!

THE ROLE OF THE SPIRIT

Two people uniting together in marriage according to Ephesians 5:18-21, should be Spirit-filled individuals. This means the Spirit of God is in charge of each life, enabling the individual to control the emotional impulses which would cause them to speak against each other.

The Holy Spirit brings restraint, saying, "There is no need to voice that right now." Or, "Before you say another word, check your attitude."

If we are Spirit-filled then we will speak to ourselves in psalms, hymns and spiritual songs, singing and making melody to the Lord. In a state of praise and worship we won't have time to be angry with our mate.

How many hours do you spend on your face thanking God for your husband or praising the Lord for your wife? When you pray, honestly go before the Father and say, "I thank you for giving me this man." Or, "I thank you for giving me this woman."

Instead, many plead, "Lord, change his heart." Or, "God, please deal with her mind."

We should be grateful, thanking God for our mate. Perhaps this is the reason many are so miserable.

Giving thanks always for all things unto God the Father in the name of our Lord Jesus Christ.
— EPHESIANS 5:20

The next verse is the clincher:

Submitting yourselves one
to another in the fear of God.
– EPHESIANS 5:20

God is reminding us there must be "giving and receiving" in a relationship. The woman isn't always right, nor is the man, yet there must be times when they come into agreement. Since there are two diverse opinions, agreement comes when each partner puts aside his or her opinion to agree on what is right for both of them.

ONE ACCORD

Concerning household matters, it should not be an area where either is looking for permission, but for mutual agreement. If we are Spirit-filled, there should not be bickering over differences of opinion.

Yes, there will be times we don't always agree, however, if the Spirit leads us, there should be harmony. This is what God desires in His house.

If we really want to see the power of God move in our household, then we must come into agreement as partners and family.

The relationship between a husband and wife should be indicative of the communion between Christ and the Church. Do you think Christ desires a bride who is always contradictory, disagreeing with Him?

This model does not make a woman a second-class citizen, or a subservient individual. It simply says that because she loves God so much, she wants to be like-minded with what His Word specifies for the relationship to be. You are also saying, "Lord because I love You, I want to come in line with your Word."

WHO IS OUR IDENTITY?

There are people who idolize their spouse, thinking he or she is the reason why they are significant. There are others who feel they must have "someone" in their life, in order to feel important. It gives them their worth and value. For that reason, many spouses put *everything* into their mate—and when that person dies, their identity is also buried. They no longer feel they exist. The Bible tells us:

...For you died, and your life is hidden with Christ in God. When Christ who is our life appears... then we will also appear with Him in glory...
−COLOSSIANS 3:3-4

Christ is our life, not our mate. We should never find our identity wrapped up in the person we marry, but rather in our Savior. Why? Because we are *whole* in Christ. No other being can substitute who we are in Him.

We must learn to be the person God made us to be and stop allowing other people to conform us to their image. Just as we should not look to others to complete us, we need to avoid expecting them to *define* us.

57

DOMINATION AND CONTROL

We often find people re-living episodes in their lives which were played out before them by their parents. There are men who marry women to recreate what they saw going on in their own household. Perhaps their mother was docile, laid back and had very little to say, if anything. Their father dominated. He really wasn't a leader, rather a dictator.

These kinds of men often seek women they can control, because that's what they lived under and witnessed first hand. Also, since their father was an authoritarian, they are determined to be just like him. I am convinced this is nothing more than a generational curse.

To view it from another angle, there are women whose mothers were dominated, and now they are determined to marry men who dominate them. Or, in certain cases it is the reverse—women whose mothers were very domineering. I believe this is done habitually, not knowingly.

Their mothers ran the family with an iron fist and everybody knew it. Therefore, they seek men who are weak and don't take their rightful position as leaders. If not broken, this becomes a perpetual cycle. Someone must be willing to end the pattern of domination and control, which is witchcraft. The Bible states:

For rebellion is as the sin of witchcraft, and stubbornness is as iniquity and idolatry. Because you have rejected the word of the Lord.
−1 SAMUEL 15:23

58

These issues are passed from one generation to another because no one has the will or determination to stand against them. This is why families keep on suffering through the same plagues.

...And the Lord passed before him and proclaimed, the Lord, the Lord God, merciful and gracious, longsuffering and abounding in goodness and truth, keeping mercy for thousands, forgiving iniquity and transgression and sin, by no means clearing the guilty, visiting the iniquity of the fathers upon the children and the children's children to the third and the fourth generation.
— EXODUS 24:6-7

Unfortunately, many homes are not predicated upon truth. Although the Church should be the pillar and foundation of such truth, it is actually made up of those same weak people. Therefore, the church has an obligation to teach, preach and demonstrate truth until it penetrates the hearts of its members. It's the only way believers will mature in the Lord.

ROUND AND ROUND!

We are often much more concerned with the serenity of the household than personal development and growth. In the process we avoid the hard realities and fail to speak to matters which are pertinent, necessary or relative to truly meeting the deeper needs of the individual God has given as our mate.

It reminds me of the phrase, "Here we go round the mulberry bush." You just blindly keep repeating the same routine every day, with neither spouse saying, "Aren't you tired of going around this bush?"

One party in the relationship must take the initiative and admit, "We can't continue like this. I'm tired of going around in circles!"

It is essential married couples learn to communicate their honest feelings to each other. You don't really have a relationship if you can't speak truth when it is called for. Instead you have an arrangement where you have agreed not to touch certain hot topics—even if they arise.

In a marital bond, both parties need to strive to become everything God said they can be. There should not be any stunting of growth because the man or woman refuses to allow the other person to be who they are. Remember, the Bible tells us:

> *For you are all sons of God through faith in Christ Jesus. For as many of you as were baptized into Christ have put on Christ. There is neither Jew nor Greek, there is neither slave nor free, there is neither male nor female; for you are all one in Christ Jesus.*
> – GALATIANS 3:26-28

In many instances a husband or wife who has more education and earns a higher salary than their spouse may feel superior and think they have a greater position in the marriage. Never forget, we are all one in Christ Jesus.

Some have allowed their marriage to function like a lottery, always waiting for the big pay off. They don't know what it is to continually "abide" in love. Jesus tells us:

> *As the Father loved me I also have loved you, abide*
> *n my love...." Continue in my love..." "...If you keep*
> *my commandments, you will abide in My Love, just as I have*
> *kept My Father's commandments and abide in His love.*
> *These things I have spoken to you, that my joy*
> *may remain in you, and that your joy may be full.*
>
> – J O H N   1 5 :   9 - 1 1

Love is a commandment; it is not an option.

There may come a time when one mate begins to outgrow the other. The one who is blossoming often has problems with the mate who is standing still. This presents irritation and agitation and calls for a return to the virtue of patience.

GIVERS AND RESPONDERS

Men must understand that biblical leadership means the man should be the greater servant in the relationship. Why? Because man was created to be a giver, and the woman was made to be a responder.

In responding there is giving. If we really have God's fervent love abiding and abounding inside, we should always be giving, and sacrificing. Therefore men, even when your spouse is not offering you what you want, you should remain faithful, and continue to give to her.

That's true leadership.

The Lord sets the example, always making sure we are supplied and have our needs met. We are His bride and because He loves us and cares so much, He is always inviting us to His bountiful table.

The Lord gives this example of servanthood:

> *Jesus called them together and said, you know that the rulers of the Gentiles lord it over them, and their high officials exercise authority over them. Not so with you...whoever wants to become great among you must be your servant, and whoever wants to be first must be your slave. Just as the Son of man did not come to be served, but to serve, and to give His life as a ransom for many.*
> – MATTHEW 20:25-28 NIV

Since you and I were created in His image, we must always be willing to serve. It's the only way to begin the process of resolving the dispute in your household. I can guarantee your spouse will respond.

MELTING THE ICE

Women, please understand a man faced with constant criticism eventually becomes dejected and gives up. The more you debase with your words, the more you demoralize him and he retreats back within himself. When that happens he no longer brings his personality home. His body is there, but his mind is far away.

Sooner or later he will spend more time at work and find every excuse to remain longer at the office. He dreads having to put the key in the ignition and drive his car home—because he knows what he has to deal with when he gets there.

No one likes to feel the ice. So, make sure there is always warmth and love in your heart when you greet your mate.

The wife needs to set the right climate in the home so her spouse can come into a place where he knows he is welcome and wanted. Make Proverbs 31 your anthem and speak with wisdom.

When you talk with your mate, love should shape your words as you appeal to the deeper instinct within the man. Remember, he is a giver by God's own creation and design—and you are to make sure you give him a reason to want to give more.

Don't criticize or put him down. Make sure what you say is not filled with friction and negativity. Since a man is looking for affirmation, he needs to have positive input.

Concerning attitude, the Bible states:

> *A quarrelsome wife is like a constant dripping*
> *on a rainy day; restraining her is like restraining*
> *the wind or grasping oil with the hand.*
> – PROVERBS 27:15-16 NIV

What a descriptive, powerful scripture! If a man attempts to hold this type of wife back, it's like trying to push back the wind or hold oil in your hand. It will slip through your fingers.

"WOW! THIS IS IT!"

If you really want to see your husband respond to you

properly, make sure you do not nag him repeatedly. If you say something and he heard you, there's no need to follow him around the house with the same criticism. You'll only encourage him to retreat to his favorite room with the remote control—or he may decide to leave the house!

Our homes are supposed to be a haven, an oasis, not a battleground.

Your abode should be a refreshing place so you can say, "Wow! This is it! I don't want to be anywhere else." With the spirit, soul, and mind at ease, you can enter the threshold and be renewed.

When building God's Kingdom, people don't need to be in a state of constant strife at home. They see enough of this when they are dealing with the world.

Let your residence be a place where you can come and lay your head on your pillow in peace.

In the words of King Solomon:

As a loving deer and a graceful doe,
let her breasts satisfy you at all times; and
always be enraptured with her love.
– PROVERBS 5:19

Women should make themselves accessible for their husbands to be refreshed. However, a man is supposed to make sure it is reciprocal. This doesn't only mean sex, because a woman would much rather have you make love to her mind before you try to make love to her body. This is what a wife desires from her husband, and I believe it is the highest form of intimacy.

IT'S ALL ABOUT HIM

In the Hebrew culture women were very subservient. In fact, a woman wasn't supposed to say anything unless asked. In the synagogue, a curtain was drawn between the sexes. The men sat on one side, the women on the other. If they wanted to know more, they would call over the curtain trying to get their husband's attention. That is living in bondage and it's not God's original plan.

We must reach the point where we truly begin to make our homes the haven God desires. It's time to stop the frivolous folly of conflict with one another and come to the place where we totally adhere to God's Word. It's all about Him.

Marriage is for the glory of God, not just for each other.

Another thing you do: You flood the Lord's altar with tears. You weep and wail because he no longer pays attention to your offerings or accepts them with pleasure from your hands. You ask "Why?" It is because the Lord is acting as the witness between you and the wife of your youth, because you have broken faith with her, though she is your partner, the wife of your marriage

65

*covenant. Has not the Lord made them one? In flesh and
spirit they are His. And why one? Because he was seeking
Godly offspring. So guard yourself in your spirit and do not
break faith with the wife of your youth, "I hate divorce,"
says the Lord God of Israel, "and I hate a man covering
himself with violence as well as with his garment," says the
Lord Almighty. So guard yourself in your spirit and do not
break faith. You have wearied the Lord with your words.
"How have we wearied him?" you ask. By saying, "All
who do evil are good in the eyes of the Lord, and he is
pleased with them" or "Where is the God of Justice?"*

– MALACHI 2: 13-17 NIV

We do not marry to have a constant bed partner, or
have a person to stroke our ego every moment of the day.
Nor do we marry to dominate. It is a union for the glory
of God.

It pleases our Heavenly Father to know we are
making every effort to resolve any and all disputes so His
joy can remain in us as we continue in His love.

CHAPTER FOUR

MAN'S DESIRE TO CONTROL

Looking at man, one might think there is nothing too complex about him. You might even comment, "If you've seen one, you've seen them all!" But, that's not the case, because in many ways, a man can be as intricate and difficult to understand as a woman.

There are different tendencies and facets to a man's life and his responses will determine his attitude and future visibility in society.

The media gives mixed signals. The male is sometimes portrayed in television or the movies as incompetent and inept, being led rather than leading. On the other hand, they are also depicted as macho, Rambo types—not needing anyone to lean on. There are men who spend countless hours attempting to live up to the picture which has been painted about them, yet it is not the image God created man to be.

Men must understand the importance of not

complicating their lives and those around them by conforming to negative societal labels. It only results in becoming the stereotypes that surround them —particularly if they have never had a positive example to follow.

When a man has never had a true male role model, his life is lived through trial and error.

By following such a path he will find himself on a journey which leads to disappointment. As scripture states:

This only have I found, God made mankind upright, but men have gone in search of many schemes.
– ECCLESIASTES 7:29 NIV

In other words, man has spent much of his time in search of what he *thought* was going to make him a powerful, visible and viable person in society. This often leads to concentration on the secular world, while ignoring the spiritual. Sadly, many men become physically able, yet spiritually inept.

A WELL-TEMPERED MAN

A man's temperament can also cause him to be unpredictable. The word "temperament" is defined as the characteristic, psychological and emotional state of an individual that tends to condition his responses to various situations in life.

The characteristics which shape a man's thoughts and feelings produce whatever his responses are going to be to life.

If secular influences have tempered a man's mind, then the majority of his thinking will be carnal in nature. The "new man," which is supposed to be the dominant factor in his life, is still immature, and his responses are also childish—yet, he will rarely acknowledge it. He would rather take the attitude, "I'm a man, and I am to be respected as such."

Men do not always experience the full range of their feelings, which is one of the reasons they are sometimes incapable of showing affection and even expressing their deepest joys or fears.

They usually don't take the time to cultivate or develop the emotional side of their life because they have been taught women are the only ones who should really express their feelings. What they don't understand is that the woman is also who they were because everything she became, Adam already was.

God took Eve out of Adam; separated her from him,

and therefore what she is, man already possessed.

Emotions were undoubtedly a part of Adam's being and early on, man showed the vile side of his character. As scripture reveals, Cain became a murderer. So, the very first actions of man were not those of love, but of hate and violence. This pattern has continued through the generations.

A man's psychological and emotional state determines how he responds to various situations in life. Men may not be as visibly emotional as women, yet they still possess a very wide range of human feelings.

A ROLLER COASTER

The Lord gave me a revelation about men who exhibit "situational" emotions. This means those who only display their feelings in certain situations. For example, if they are watching their favorite football or basketball team on television, a variety of reactions are on display.

As their team goes through ebbs and flows, they are on a roller coaster, and the viewer is right there riding with them. They go from Mount Everest to Death Valley.

If the game gets tight, men are perched on the edge of their seat. When the team scores or loses the ball in a tense moment, they shout loudly! If they lose the game at the buzzer to a guy on the opposing team who usually can't throw a boulder in the ocean, they may sink into the sofa, stunned. They sit there wallowing in the depths of depression because their team lost. Yet they tell everybody, "I'm not emotional!"

The problem is: some men find it difficult to share their feelings with another person. In order for them to become vulnerable and transparent, they must develop trust.

If a man makes a decision to marry a woman, he supposedly is doing so because he trusts her with his life. This being the case, he should not find it awkward or difficult being totally transparent. He must learn to express anxieties and his fear of failure. The trouble is he has never learned how to properly vent his feelings.

Some men are known as charmers because they have a unique way with words and know exactly how to present themselves—without there being genuine feeling or emotion.

It's difficult for men to hear the truth about themselves, preferring not to deal with it. Plus, no husband wants a wife to expose private details concerning him that are not positive. However, to maintain a successful marriage, he must become transparent and remove the walls between himself and his mate. He should openly and honestly discuss anything with her which may be detrimental to their relationship.

CRYING TIMES

It is important for a man to build his circle of friends by allowing others to share their insights. To illustrate the importance of being open and transparent, let's look at what the apostle Paul said to the elders of Ephesus:

When they arrived he said to them, you know how I lived the whole time I was with you, from the first day I came into the province of Asia. I served the Lord with great humility and with tears, although I was severely tested by the plot of the Jews. You know that I have not hesitated to preach anything that would be helpful to you but have taught you publicly and from house to house.

– ACTS 20:18-20

Many believe a man should be hard, coarse and rough. But the apostle Paul stated he had no problem being humble and crying in their midst. He also faced trials and tests.

Though he had gone through some difficult, trying times, Paul was humble and compassionate, yet remained accessible. He lived an open life in public, going from house to house, providing for those under his care. That's a man of God!

Most men desire to maintain complete control of their neatly ordered world, so that any demonstration of 'weakness' will not be discovered.

Some husbands dominate their spouse to ensure the woman understands the "boundaries." They insist she must know what she can and cannot say, and what she can and cannot *do*. There are certain topics which have been predetermined as "gray areas"—being off limits for discussion. He puts up a "No Trespassing" sign and tells her, "I'm sorry, we can't go there!"

A COVER FOR WEAKNESS

As men order women's lives, what really happens is they reveal their own weaknesses. Some are quick to point the finger at their spouse and tell her what she did wrong. They may say "It's not my fault things are like this, because all you need to know is I am right."

The wife is then seen as a person who can't think and has no input. She must listen while he speaks.

If he is allowed to control the marriage in such a manner, what he is really demonstrating is manipulation. Sadly, he is communicating, "Just be here. I don't want to hear what God gave you for me.

And when I ask you to do something, do it. When I want your opinion I'll ask for it!"

Many men do not allow themselves to open up and expose some of the wounds in their own life. They hide them very carefully to ensure their weaknesses are not discovered.

Men are predominantly performance oriented; which means they always make sure they are viewed as men who can produce something.

This makes them feel they are in control. In the words of the apostle Paul:

But He said to me, "My grace is sufficient for you, for my power is made perfect in weakness." Therefore I will boast all the more gladly about my weaknesses, so that Christ's power may rest on me. That is why, for Christ's sake I delight in weaknesses, in insults, in hardships, in persecutions, in difficulties. For when I am weak, then I am strong.
– 2 CORINTHIANS 12:9-10 NIV

God does not ask a man to walk around acting like Superman—showing himself to be this strong, virile individual. Instead, the Lord is attempting to get men to admit their weaknesses. The Apostle Paul writes he would rather boast about his shortcomings than stand up and brag how powerful he is.

When men finally acquiesce to the point of admitting weaknesses, then the power of Christ will rest upon them.

The kind of strength all men should pursue is the might and force of God's Son. At some point a man's abilities will end, yet through the power of Christ, and the anointing of the Holy Spirit he too can say, "When I am weak, then am I strong."

It is a natural instinct for a man to want to prove his manhood. However, the need to control and show power can also cause a man to justify his wrongdoings. Since there is a desire to be in control, they often find excuses and reasons to blame others for their actions.

WHO IS AT FAULT?

Cain is undoubtedly a picture of the first man who desired to get control at any cost (Genesis 4). This son of Adam was extremely angry because God did not accept his offering. Like most men, rather than admit there was something wrong with his actions, he transferred the blame to his brother Abel.

Just as Cain saw Abel as the object of his failure, today there are men who see women as the cause of their downfall. They feel if they had not married, they would probably be further ahead in life (The Adam Syndrome).

This reverts back to the idea of performance orientation, because men elevate their desire to flawlessly execute in this world while not appreciating the gift God gave them. When relationship challenges arise, many men no longer see their wife as a treasured *gift*.

So, Cain rose up against Abel, and slew him. Today, many men do the same to their wives. Oh, she's still alive physically, but they've suffocated her spirit and her zest to live and be productive. They have snuffed out her affections and feelings by stomping on her heart and not giving her room to breathe and grow.

How can such men call their wife a "partner" when there is no partnership or protection?

Because men feel a need to dominate and exert power, they often find it difficult to relate to the biblical instructions for them to dominate the earth, not each other. Men controlled by society (whether by domineering parents, friends or employers), often desire a position of control in the home to the point of oppressing their mate. Remember, a man is the foundation of the home, and if the foundation is faulty, then everything else is at risk.

The head of every household should desire to build a family on solid rock.

THE BLAME GAME

Men must stop finding justification for the things they do wrong—or their inability or unwillingness to take their rightful place in the home, church and society. Man's desire for power and praise is nothing new. Neither is his tendency to pass the blame for his actions to others and justify wrong behavior.

Scripture shows us in Genesis 4:16-23, the example of Lamech, the great, great, great grandson of Cain. Lamech killed a man, and then excused his actions by saying to his wives that if God said Cain would be avenged seven times, then he would be avenged seventy- sevenfold. Lamech tried to rationalize his wrongdoing the same way his ancestor tried to justify the murder of his brother: by passing the blame.

THE CRY FOR RECOGNITION

The desire for power in most men is strong and they like to be recognized and praised. Do you remember "Butch" when you were growing up? Or "Spike"—or whatever his name was. He was the tough guy in the neighborhood who acted macho, talked rough and seemed fearless.

This type of behavior exhibits itself publicly because of man's desire for recognition. However, when Butch was alone or with his family, he wasn't always so full of bravado.

Parents who fail to give their sons guidance and a solid foundation in life will produce a mean-spirited, aggressive, domineering temperament in young men. It often requires "outside" teachers to shape these lives.

Once learned behavior becomes a part of our psyche it is almost impossible to unlearn. In the case of Cain, the knowledge he acted upon has perpetuated itself through the generations. Some men were spoiled by their mothers, which created within them the attitude they should always be catered to.

Men shouldn't want their children to emulate them unless they portray the image of God.

"IN CONTROL"

Another facet of man's power concerns dress codes. We've all had some contact with what society terms as "power dressing." You wear certain clothing to display a desired persona in order to achieve a hoped-for level of respect. For example, a dark suit exemplifies power; an expensive, coordinated ensemble, with leather briefcase included, represents authority and competence. When a man is presented in such a manner, he is exalted and celebrated as a person of substance who is "in charge."

Power not only has its own dress and behavioral codes, it has a unique vocabulary. If a man is going to be one who portrays power and control, he has to be able to speak the language of the environment. When he "walks the walk and talks the talk,"everyone in that arena sees him as "a man in the know" who is capable and competent. This is their man of influence, who demands respect and commands an audience. When he speaks, they want to hear what he has to say. This type of power can easily take control of his very being.

It's easy to become accustomed to being "number one" and having your public image celebrated and venerated. The problem arises, however, when we can no longer hold the position. This "fall from grace" causes many men to do whatever is necessary to remove the person who has replaced them as "top dog." But who is that man when the spotlight is turned off and he can no longer hear the cheers of the crowd?

VICTORY OVER VANITY

Remember Cain's offering! When a man lives up to this type of power, gained by learned behavior without a sound spiritual foundation, the spirit of Cain easily overcomes him. He learns to do whatever it takes to maintain his position in society and often passes these values (or lack of them) on to the next generation.

God has favor for all of us, and more than one offering is acceptable, as long as you bring the *right* gift.

When men learn to exhibit the type of behavior that is pleasing to God and in line with His Word, they learn true power.

Men must stop trying to give the Lord what they *think* He should have, and instead present God what He truly desires.

Forget trying to move everybody out of the way just to achieve fleeting power. It's time to focus on dying to self-centered desires so God's power can shine through you.

Do nothing out of selfish ambition or vain conceit, but in humility consider others better than yourselves...
— PHILIPPIANS 2:3 NIV

This means a husband should care for his spouse before himself. After God the Father, his wife must be the first priority in his life, not his status or position in the world. His ego and image, or how his "fans" see him, are unimportant.

OIL AND WATER DON'T MIX

Most men end up with a distorted perspective of the male/female assignments because of the tendency to mingle secular perceptions with spiritual instructions. They fuse the corporate world with church, and they stir secular knowledge or humanism in with that which is spiritual. This is like trying to mix oil and water; it won't work! God says:

> *Therefore come out from among them, and*
> *be separate, says the Lord. Do not touch what*
> *is unclean, and I will receive you.*
> – 2 CORINTHIANS 6:17 NIV

There are those who set themselves up in questionable personal situations knowing full well that evil company can corrupt good morals. In other words, if you hang out with people who don't have a heart for God, not only will you look like them, you will soon start acting like them.

Let's look at two types of power. One is gained through fear or punishment, the other gained through love.

The first type of power, (the fear factor, or carrying

a big stick) is how many men gain control over women. They withhold themselves emotionally and in an attitude of silence or neglect when the woman does not act the way they feel she should. Attempts by the woman to communicate are met with silence or anger. Volatile, hostile, and rebellious are words to describe how he reacts to her efforts. This is her "punishment" and his means of gaining control.

Men may go to the extreme of withdrawing their physical presence as a penalty—they stay out late, or perhaps don't come home at all. This type of behavior is their quest for power.

The woman is now in fear of doing or saying anything because she does not want to be punished. If the pattern is allowed to continue, the man literally becomes her master. Unfortunately, even in the body of Christ, at times the abuse is physical. We try to hide it, but it is true nevertheless.

CHERISH IS THE WORD

Praise God, there is another approach. This is where strength is gained through love. This type of power is God-ordained, effective and enduring. The Word counsels:

...Husbands ought to love their own wives as their own bodies...He, who loves his wife, loves himself.

For no one ever hated his own flesh, but nourishes and cherishes it, just as the Lord does the church.
— EPHESIANS 5:28-29 NIV

This passage tells men they are to spend their time loving their spouse. According to the Word, the more you cherish her, the more power you will have.

If you give a woman love she will respond in kind. That is her makeup—to give back what she receives.

Men who exist to be in control may desire a subservient wife who lives only to do his bidding. However, when this happens they lose out on the true qualities a woman possesses which are meant to bless a man's life. As a result, the things that would cause him to succeed are being stymied and he cannot achieve his full potential—nor his true, God-ordained power.

"I'M JUST FINE!"

Men are competitive but not always confrontational. They endure physical pain and put up a good front publicly, but many of them have great difficulty dealing one-on-one concerning emotional issues. Many are so afraid of facing the truth they would rather tolerate suffering in their bodies than have anyone (even their doctors) see their discomfort or distress.

If you ask most men how they are feeling, they answer, "I'm just fine."

The problem with this type of attitude is that many of these men end up like Cain. When the façade of power falls apart, and they realize they can't be accepted as they wish, they start an uprising.

However, men need to understand that once they display this "Cain spirit," their mate normally withdraws. Most women recognize the need for dominance and excessive control in men, and will back away to avoid succumbing to this control.

THE BASIS OF LOVE

Having to function in the world's system causes men to become performance and goal oriented. A woman's true love for man, however, should not be based on his position in the corporate world. Most women evaluate their love for a man on how he loves her.

When two believers come together in fulfillment of God's plan for marriage, the woman bases her love for the man on how he loves God and her. She is not looking for him to be a millionaire or the CEO of a company, if that's not what God has envisioned for him.

As long as he continues to be her loving, gentle, kind, compassionate, caring, concerned, prayerful, spiritual husband, she will submit to him and nurture him, physically, emotionally and mentally—and if he happens to be a millionaire as well, it wouldn't be bad!

Women desire men who are willing to fulfill their roles, as provider, protector and priest in the home, so they may respond with respect and love. God will take care of the rest.

UNTAPPED POTENTIAL

I have encountered men who act as if their mate would be nothing without them and their success in society is responsible for her being. They do not realize that they were able to climb high because she was taking care of the home and stabilizing the ladder.

A woman is a wealth of untapped potential, waiting for a man to give to her, so she can shape his ideas and dreams by her response.

Our materialistic culture directly contributes to a man's image of himself. Women are measured by their eloquence, grace, beauty and charm, while a man is measured by his status, power and money. That's how society keeps score. It places false values on us, and unfortunately, we conform to the distorted image. In our world, money may be able to buy authority or power, but it can't purchase real happiness.

No one from the east or the west, or from
the desert can exalt a man. But it is God who judges,
He brings one down, He exalts another.
— PSALM 75:6-7 NIV

True power comes when a man seeks God's face and learns what he needs to do to strengthen his weaknesses. He must become his own CFO (Chief Faith Intercessor), until God brings results.

Whatever a man sows he shall reap. Men, if you sow a poor attitude, greed and lack of respect for your mate, you will garner the same harvest.

Learn to face who you are so you will be able to honor women and see them as equal partners. When this happens, your heart's desire will not be to dominate your spouse, but to protect and provide for her in accordance with the Will of God.

When men reach the stage of maturity where they are able to express their deepest innermost feelings, confronting issues head on, then and only then will they begin to fulfill their God ordained role in their marriage.

CHAPTER FIVE

WOMAN OF
INFLUENCE

T*o the woman He said, I will greatly increase
your pains in childbearing. In pain you will give
birth to children. Your desire will be for your
husband, and he will rule over you.*
— GENESIS 3:16 NIV

At this pivotal time in history, the challenges of being
a woman are far greater than ever known. Shortly before
the industrial revolution most women were house-
wives—and their husbands were self-employed farmers.
Because the wife was alongside her husband, she was his
helpmate on the farm while raising the children.

Then, when factories began to open worldwide, men
found employment outside of agriculture—placing great
burdens and pressures on women left at home.

As world wars and advances in technology took
place, things changed even more. Increasing numbers of

men were going off to battle or working away from the homestead. The death toll of international conflict was extremely high, which left even more women alone—many at a young age—to take care of the home and raise families, often without any male assistance.

Next came inflation, leading to higher living costs and women were forced to fulfill a still different role.

This brings us to the present day where many women, because of divorce and other reasons, are left to manage without help. They provide for the children and make sure they are nurtured and properly cared for. At the same time, they have to maintain a balance in their lives, setting aside time for themselves and their own interests.

Today, millions of women are pursuing careers while still trying to manage a household. This adds even more pressure on a woman's life—which also shapes her personality and leads to more independence.

Having to endure on her own under stress, she develops a self-sufficient nature and, in some instances, a superior attitude. Should a woman marry, this air of independence often causes division and strife between men and women, especially when a man becomes threatened by her self-reliance and in many instances intimidated by the strong belief she has in herself.

An Independent Dependent

In truth, the Almighty intended for the woman to be an "independent dependent." He gave the mandate to the male to provide for the woman. She was designated to be his helpmate, nurturing and taking care of the home, while the man makes provision for her and the children. She was designed to operate on her own as his dependant, but never as an independent entity.

The act of rebellion in the Garden established the woman's freedom to choose. Although she was aware of the mandate God gave to the man, and knew her role, she overrode it and operated separately from her husband. The spirit of rebellion born by that act exists in some women today.

WHO IS THE SOURCE?

A spirit of independence can cause a woman to run out from under the protective covering of the man.

God made provision for a woman to be protected, not the "protector."

Today's society insists on birthing and breeding a culture of women who are totally self-reliant. This learned nature is so prevalent that even in marriage, they want to be independent. They shun the concept of a man leading them. They have been raised to stand on their own two feet.

Scripture says women are to look to their husband as

their source. The Bible declares, *"...the man is the head of the woman..."* (1 Corinthians 11:3 NIV). The word "head" does not mean lord and master. It actually signifies "source."

Man is supposed to be the source of provision to the woman, and she is not to be independent of him.

God's Word also tells us:

> *In that day seven women will take hold of one man and say, "We will eat our own food and provide our own clothes; only let us be called by your name. Take away our disgrace."*
> – ISAIAH 4:1

Today we have a significant number of men dying from street violence, wars and AIDS. Many more are addicted to alcohol and drugs, and are dead spiritually— unaware of their role in the family and society according to God's mandate.

THE COMPETITION FACTOR

There are vast numbers of women who desire to be married, yet place their career ahead of marriage and the call to be a man's "helper."

Some are so busy climbing the corporate ladder they have forgotten their call to nurture. So they carry their independent spirit into the management of the household. As far as they are concerned it's their money and they can call the shots as they please.

When this happens, the woman is perpetuating the independent spirit established by Eve.

Society has created a competition between men and women when there is absolutely no need to compete. God made both equal from the very beginning of time. Here is what the Creator said to the world's first human inhabitants:

> *God blessed them and said to them, "Be fruitful and increase in number; fill the earth and subdue it. Rule over the fish of the sea and the birds of the air and over every living creature that moves on the ground."*
> —GENESIS 1:28 NIV

Woman was given a state of equality when Eve allowed the devil to make her believe that she was missing something. As the Bible records:

> *"...so when the woman saw that the tree was good for food. she took of its fruit and ate. She also gave to her husband with her, and he ate."*
> – GENESIS 3:6

Even in this act of rebellion, the woman recognized that what was in her was also in the man—and she gave him what she felt he needed.

Today, women are being raised to feel they have certain "rights." Because of such thinking, women sometimes look at their husbands with contempt in their eyes and hearts. They feel they are unequal and must give up their rights to live in a "man's world." Many women believe this is unfair.

As a believer in the Lord Jesus Christ all of our rights are supposed to be relinquished—given over to the Almighty for His handling and safekeeping. If we are going to follow Christ, we should deny ourselves and walk with Him.

YOU'RE A TEMPLE

There is no need for women to feel trapped, ensnared or in bondage. Nor do they need to put up a struggle for equal rights. As a believer, we give up our rights and allow Christ to be the Lord of our life.

The point of our justification should be Christ. The apostle Paul is speaking directly to you and me when he says:

> *...do you not know that your body is the temple of the Holy Spirit who is in you, whom you have from God, and you are not your own? For you were bought at a price; therefore glorify God in your body and in your spirit, which are God's.*
> – 1 CORINTHIANS 6:19-20

If women look for satisfaction from above there will be no need for them to be overly concerned of what their mate is or is not doing. When God is truly the Head of your life and is your total sufficiency, then it's all about Him—and no one else!

A Spirit of Arrogance

Without question we should live confidently, but the spirit of independence can also produce arrogance. Remember, women have egos—even if they are not as dominant a factor as in men.

It is the woman's independent spirit which leads to a display of haughtiness and intolerance. Arrogance is defined as having an inflated sense of self. When this is present, women literally exalt themselves above their spouse.

Those who are overly independent exhibit a spirit of self-pride, then wonder why their mate is not as attentive to them as she would like him to be. They don't realize their attitude pushes him away and is a deterrent to his performance as a provider and protector.

You're the Crown

Some women have the capacity to make decisions in a precise manner in the marketplace, but are unable to use wisdom in dealing with situations in the home. Others, however, become even more arrogant and their independent spirit grows stronger.

When this happens, instead of the woman celebrating her mate, she will only tolerate him, because she has set herself up above him. She does not see the need to follow or submit to him as the head, because instead of viewing herself as his helper, she is convinced she is his superior.

Women must realize that intelligence does not automatically qualify a person to lead.

Scripture declares:

> *An excellent wife is the crown of her husband...*
> — PROVERBS 12:4

A woman, as a crown to her mate,
cannot be lost in his identity or personality.
She is a symbol of his authority.

When a person wears a crown, its appearance and position is always important.

Scripture also tells us, *"... she who causes shame is like rottenness in his bones"* (Proverbs 12:4) So if a woman possesses the wrong attitude, the Bible says she becomes an embarrassment to the man's life.

Men are grieved when their spouse refuses to be their crown.

NURTURING WORDS

Although women have a need to express themselves verbally, they must ensure that their conversation is edifying to their spouse. Husbands must also learn to appreciate their wives' need to talk. However, women need to temper their conversation with wisdom according to Proverbs 31:26.

Women must bring themselves into the presence of God and speak His words, rather than simply opening their mouths to fulfill their need to converse.

If you must chide or correct your husband, avoid a provoking or vexing manner. Remember, man is a warrior and he does not retreat when a battle is engaged. You are called to nurture him, so bathe your words in love, respect and wisdom.

Men are looking for affirmation and agreement. They are also searching for help and information to complete their thoughts so they can make quality decisions which will benefit their entire family.

...for the husband is the head of the wife, as also Christ is the head of the church; and He is the Savior of the body. Therefore, just as the church is subject to Christ, so let the wives be to their own husbands in everything.
— EPHESIANS 5:23-24 NIV

If there is going to be a last word, or a final pronouncement, it doesn't belong to the woman. This does not mean a man can try to persuade her into doing something ungodly. A woman is well within her rights to refuse anything that is against God's Will and Word. A woman, however, should intercede for her husband to receive from God so he can make divinely blessed decisions.

THE "SILENT TREATMENT"

In most instances a woman is well aware of the influence she has over a man. She knows her capabilities, and strengths and has carefully observed the weaknesses of man. So she understands exactly what is necessary to get her way.

I'm not talking about sexual favor, rather how women exhibit certain attitudes to achieve a desired reaction. Despite their need to talk, they are also masters of the "silent treatment."

There are many women who don't like to be outdone. If it seems a man is getting the upper hand, they will do whatever is necessary to balance the scales.

In the Old Testament there is a story about King Ahab and his wife, Jezebel, who ran the house. Usually when you find a woman in charge of the household, she's an independent individual who does her own thing, while her husband tends to his business. You rarely see the man and woman together in this situation—and when they are, she is usually giving him advice on how to run his life.

The children come to her for instruction and guidance. The father can be sitting right there, and they'll walk past him to talk to her. This "head" has no influence in his own home. Even on the outside people know the woman is in charge. She makes all of the decisions, and treats her husband as if he's incompetent.

MICHAL'S HAUGHTY SPIRIT

There's another woman in history who is seldom mentioned, but I want to call your attention to her life.

Michal was King David's first bride—and later his restored wife. She was the daughter of King Saul and possessed a haughty spirit. Here is how scripture describes her feelings:

Now as the ark of the Lord came into the City of David, Michal, Saul's daughter, looked through a window and saw King David leaping and whirling before the Lord, and she despised him in her heart.
– 2 SAMUEL 6:16

David was praising God, but because of Michal's prideful spirit and concern for what other people might think, she resented him worshiping the Lord.

If a man feels his position is being threatened, he will usually respond with contempt. Or, if he surmises you are attempting to usurp "his authority" and move him out of the position of headship, it usually leads to rebellion. Why? Because he knows according to God's law he should be the head of the wife.

When David returned to bless his household, Michal came out to meet him and said:

How glorious was the king of Israel today, uncovering himself today in the eyes of his servants, as one of the base fellows shamelessly uncovers himself!
– 2 SAMUEL 6:20

97

David had disrobed himself, dancing with abandon before the Lord, and his wife, looking out her window, became upset with his behavior. She didn't try to understand what David was doing. All she knew was the king, her husband, was in public wearing only a loincloth!

David responded, "I was before the Lord who (and not your father) chose me to be the ruler over Israel. Therefore, I will play music before the Lord."

The warrior inside David had been awakened by her anger. In essence, he was saying, "Don't challenge me on this, or I'll become even more undignified."

He knew the people saw him as their king—a worshiper; not as a naked man.

THE "ORDER OF THINGS"

God is not happy with a woman who attempts to control her husband. In the beginning, the Creator established the order for families. He gave directions to Adam, and when Eve broke the order of things, God told her He would greatly multiply her sorrow in birth. This "order" is confirmed in the Word:

Wives, in the same way be submissive to your husbands so that, if any of them do not believe the Word, they may be won over without words by the behavior of their wives....

– 1 PETER 3:1-4

Rather than exemplifying ungodly behavior, women should win men over by their attitude and actions. Their conduct and fear of God needs to shape their spirit in ways which lead husbands to take their God-given position as head of the family.

ATTENTIVE AND AFFECTIONATE

Womanly adornment is not merely outward arranging of the hair, wearing gold or putting on fine apparel.

The hidden, uncorrupted portion of a woman's heart is very precious to God.

Instead of being abrasive, abusive and cold, women are fashioned to be gentle, loving, attentive and affectionate. If a wife opens her mouth with wisdom while communicating with her husband, she will be able to reap God's results in her marriage.

It's natural for women to be resentful if their husband is not sharing his thoughts. They react coldly to perceived neglect or if they feel they are only included when their spouse feels its convenient. So they retaliate by keeping their thoughts to themselves.

Remember, the woman is created to be a helper. When she is unable to fulfill her role, she feels stifled because of the creative ideas she wants to share. Feeling unnecessary or unwanted creates a strain on the marriage.

It's "Due"

Certain women respond to their husband based on specific issues they grew up with. For example, a wife may have been part of a family which did not display any signs of physical touching and little verbal communication.

Perhaps the husband is unaware of her upbringing and when he places his hand on her, she may respond inappropriately. What happens next is that some women withhold themselves sexually, physically and emotionally from their husbands.

This defensiveness can eventually become another form of manipulation or intimidation for the purpose of domination and control. Most men will give in so they can have relief and release in their life.

Here is what God's Word counsels:

Let the husband render to his wife the affection due her, and likewise also the wife to her husband.
— 1 CORINTHIANS 7:3

Read that verse again and see the words "affection due her."

Wives, you are not supposed to enter your bedroom every night complaining of a headache or Delilah may come around attempting to take your place.

I fully realize there are times women are faced with physical and emotional conditions which impact their chemical balance. Even so, God desires for the wife to make every effort to give the husband the affection which is "due."

When women withhold themselves from their husbands as a means of control it can cause men to become weak to temptation. What may have been perceived as neglect could become a reality. Far too often, husbands gravitate to areas where they feel appreciated and in charge. This has led to involvement outside the home—including extra-marital affairs.

A MENDED MARRIAGE

There is a "little girl" residing inside most women who is afraid of being hurt or appearing vulnerable. However, if husbands are to feel valued by their wives, there must be a mutual sharing and respect. With open communication and trust, men will be encouraged to fulfill their God-ordained role as provider and head of household.

When women give their husbands honor and esteem they will almost always respond with affection, cooperation and take responsibility for their actions,

Communication is vital. Men and women ought to speak with wisdom and say the things that are going to help and edify each other. A marital relationship should exemplify a husband and wife loving one another. It is all about two people understanding their roles.

It's time to stop looking at what a man or woman is *not* and understand what they are called to be. If each fulfills their assignment, God becomes involved and brings their purpose to fruition.

If either party makes a wrong turn, apologize, accept the consequences and make the necessary correction. Don't look for alibis. It's too easy to say, "The devil made me do it!"

When women begin to take responsibility for their actions and allow the fear of God to shape their spirit, men will respond positively. With the Lord's help, the result is a mended marriage.

There is no doubt a woman possesses the innate ability to help a man become all the Lord desires him to be—she just has to use her "influence" properly.

CHAPTER SIX

STRIKING THE RIGHT CHORD

Nevertheless, neither is man independent of woman, nor woman independent of man, in the Lord. For as woman came from man, even so man also comes through woman; but all things are from God.

1 CORINTHIANS 11:11-12

Every believer in the Lord Jesus Christ must be committed to the fulfillment of God's purpose in the earth. According to Genesis 1, the Almighty wants us to be able to have *rulership*—governorship here on this planet. And there was a certain way He prescribed it.

The Creator declared, "I will make man." Then, aware man needed a helper, said, "I will make woman."

Following this union, God ordained there eventually to be a nation that would totally surrender in obedience to His holy and sovereign command. Even though this did not happen, it does not negate God's purpose for man and woman. The Almighty still expects us to have dominion on the earth.

Here is the Lord's instruction:

Now therefore, if you will indeed
obey My voice and keep My covenant.
– EXODUS 19:5-6

When God uses the word "covenant," He is saying, "I have made an agreement with you which you are to keep."

As scripture records, the Lord continues, "Then you shall be a special treasure to Me above all people; for all the earth is Mine." "And you shall be to Me a kingdom of priests and a holy nation. These are the words which you shall speak to the children of Israel."

Today, because we are Abraham's seed, we inherit the same covenant. This being the case, we have a responsibility to initiate a *Holy* nation—because it pleases our Father.

How is this accomplished? Through man and woman, and in particular, husbands and wives. You see, God created a marriage covenant, and He will not change this agreement.

ENCOURAGING, INSPIRING

Marriage is supposed to be a harmonious blend of two people's lives that will ultimately bring God's kingdom to the earth. It means the melody in both the man's and woman's life are designed to come together and create a beautiful symphony.

When the world views a husband and wife, they should see a symphony that's being played out in both lives.

The sound of this union should be sweet and soothing, comforting and inspiring. Yet, this only results when there is a melodic blend of both persons. Their relationship must reflect matching notes and they should never desire to live in dissension where two notes clash.

The moment it sounds like we are out of key, we should take whatever steps necessary to get back in tune to prevent sounds of noise and confusion.

"TWO SHALL BECOME ONE"

What will result from the absence of a real melody in two people's lives? Chaos— and ultimately destruction! There are times when two spouses living under the same roof don't speak the same language because there's no merging of their "notes." They need to re-read this instruction from scripture:

For we are members of His body, of His flesh and of His bones. For this reason a man shall leave his father and mother and be joined to his wife, and the two shall become one flesh.
— EPHESIANS 5:30-31

105

When this harmony occurs, two separate notes are no longer heard, and neither will you distinguish the sound of one note louder than the other. The music emanating from the couple is so beautiful to the ear, and to one's sight, people will long to be in their presence.

Married couples must be committed to the long-term work of complementing each other, rather than fighting differences.

Ask any orchestra conductor and you will learn that creating a symphonic masterpiece involves tremendous time and practice. Unfortunately, most people entering marriage have no concept of the work involved to make it successful. The basic problem is both parties come to a relationship with independent spirits which have not been trained to merge with each other.

ELIMINATING THE "SOUR NOTES"

In the past they were able to live a certain lifestyle on their own, not concerned with making room for anyone else. However, no matter how indifferent they may be at times, they must find a way to make their lives a melody. The commitment is a long-term effort which should begin even before taking your vows at an altar.

Entering into such a covenant will prevent some of those "sour notes" we see and hear in marriages. This requires building a relationship day after day, month after month and year after year. It involves small details: an encouraging word, a gentle touch, a loving smile.

Instead of weakening the foundation, you are to build and fortify each other. Whatever his or her deficiencies may be, you are always to complement and be supportive. Regardless of the valleys your spouse may go through, you are committed to lifting and sharing the burden so the melody will ring out once more.

Even in the most distraught and overwhelming circumstances, you must decide you will not allow your mate to falter or fail. You will *comfort* instead of *confront*.

AN EXTREME MAKE-OVER?

Yes, it takes time and effort to make a difference in a positive manner rather than constant blaming or complaining, "We are so different."

Of course you come from separate backgrounds with unique mind-sets, attitudes and world views. A marriage, however involves consciously working at those differences until there is total unity in the home.

The Lord does not put a partner in your life for you to perform an "extreme make-over." Instead, you are to prepare for a lifetime of making changes together with the help of God and the power of His Holy Spirit.

*Husbands and wives must commit
to a perpetual marital agreement which
flows like a perpetual rhythm.*

Marriage is not a solo performance. You know immediately when only one person is playing a tune. Sure, there are days when we need our quiet time, however if one spouse continually plays alone they will become weary of hearing their own tune. With love and encouragement, eventually the other person will come back to the keyboard ready and willing to play.

Make sure there is a dual rhythm in your lives which reflects your daily flow. It should be in unison—and perpetual.

There are moments when one mate loses his or her song and becomes frustrated when the other person is still whistling along. Just as misery loves company, that person may try to interrupt or stop the flow. When this happens, determine in your heart you are going to rejoice and not allow anything to steal your joy.

Yes, it's possible to live under the same roof and keep our happiness intact. It happens when we love one another "no matter what."

CATCHING THE VISION

As long as you have a perpetual rhythm, there will be

a perpetual agreement. At times we may have to agree to disagree—that we don't see eye to eye on certain issues. Hopefully, the melody is still there. You can pray and discuss it later when the timing is right.

Listen to the advice given by Paul:

> *Therefore, if there is any consolation in Christ, if any comfort of love, if any fellowship of the Spirit, if any affection and mercy, fulfill my joy by being like minded, having the same love, being of one accord, of one mind.*
>
> *– PHILIPPIANS 2:1-2*

Every couple should seek to be united in purpose and labor. Have something to agree upon and have repeated conversations concerning what you intend to accomplish. Together, set goals, design a strategy and establish a plan which moves you closer to your target every day. It is one of the keys to a successful marriage.

A man must have a vision for his home and share it with his wife. When she catches that same dream, her daily work becomes meaningful. I believe a woman cannot correctly flow in her rhythm unless her husband gives her something specific to move toward. The reverse is also true. A man cannot be in sync with his own rhythm if his wife doesn't help him.

Before coming together for a common purpose and goal, both spouses must make certain they are using what God has given them as skills, abilities and anointing. Ask the Lord for His guidance since it is His objective which sets the precedent. Then start moving toward the prize together!

A COMMON PURPOSE

It's impossible to overemphasize being united in purpose. One mate should never entertain a goal which takes him or her outside the boundaries of what you decided to accomplish as a team. Remember, you are to be in agreement and laboring together.

I have met young couples who have practically nothing in common except they are madly in love with each other. That is wonderful, yet they need to have a common purpose to expand their horizons. It promotes the opportunity to discuss things outside the realm of your personal desires.

Always keep in mind the fact there needs to be a harmonious blend of likes and dislikes. A man may enjoy football and his wife doesn't, yet she chooses to watch the games with him. Likewise, a man may not relish shopping, but he joins his wife to keep the rhythm flowing.

You must share common interests outside of the bedroom. If sex is the only thing you enjoy, you will soon learn it takes much more to have a successful marriage. Spend time getting to know the kind of music and books you both appreciate. Inquire about your mate's aspirations and the things you both cherish. Otherwise your conversations will be short and the length of your marriage may be shorter!

YOUR SOLID FOUNDATION

Above all else, a husband and wife must commit to putting Christ first in their lives. Both parties should seek to be anchored in the Lord, giving Him first place.

One partner should not be leaning more toward spiritual matters than the other. Each needs to have a solid foundation in the Word—the bedrock of a healthy marriage.

Melodies between mates are interrupted when one is a God chaser, while the other chases God away! This is an issue which should be settled before rings and vows are exchanged.

Women, your desire to be married must be matched by your fervor to make sure Christ will be the head of your home—leading and guiding you through life. If not, your ship lies in shallow waters. Secular beliefs have no place in the covenant relationship God established in the beginning of time.

Not only must Christ be fully anchored in you, make sure you offer your mate what you are hearing from Christ. Share what comes through your spirit, not your flesh. That's what produces the real symphony.

EQUAL BEFORE THE LORD

Let me direct your attention to a unique couple spoken of in scripture:

Greet Priscilla and Aquila, my fellow workers in Christ Jesus, who risked their own necks for my life, to whom not

only I give thanks, but also all the churches of the Gentiles.
Likewise greet the church that is in their house.
— ROMANS 16:3-5

Aquila and Priscilla were totally surrendered to the Lordship of Christ. The Bible speaks of them at least six different times, and on three occasions Priscilla is mentioned first; and at three other times Aquila is mentioned first.

Their names are unique. Priscilla means "just an old fashioned girl." And Aquila's name means "eagle." What a interesting blend! Imagine an old fashioned young woman being led by a soaring eagle.

Priscilla had no problem doing things God's way because she knew she was being led by a man who had a vision. Notice how God saw her as being equal to Aquila, because both had surrendered to the Lord.

Most important, they were willing to risk their lives to ensure Paul's well-being. The Bible also says they were in agreement to use their home as a church and were committed to the furtherance of the gospel.

As a result, Aquila and Priscilla's sorrows were cut in half, and their joy doubled.

There's no room for the devil to
enter relationships when there is a serious
mutual commitment to Christ.

MULTIPLYING YOUR JOY

In marriage, when both parties are surrendered to the Lord, they immediately correct mistakes which could have a negative impact on their relationship. Their approach to settling the matter will not be the result of their own intellect, but through the Word of God and the guidance of the Holy Spirit. They take every situation to the Lord in prayer, knowing He has the answer.

By releasing every problem to the Father, sorrow is subtracted and happiness is multiplied. That's when we begin to experience the joy of the Lord.

When marriages are under the Lordship of Christ, sorrow may enter, but if they know how to agree with the Word, it cannot remain.

It's not uncommon for a husband or wife to say, "You're selfish. All you think about is yourself!"

That changes when both parties are submitted to the Lord and practice His admonitions to "love one another," and "pray one for the other."

When the Bible tells us "to agree quickly with your adversary," at times that may include our spouse. Yet, when Christ is truly Lord of everything, living in agreement becomes our natural lifestyle.

"BLAMELESS" BEFORE GOD

Here is an example of the kind of people God is looking for in marriage:

There was in the days of Herod the king of Judea, a certain priest named Zacharias. His name was Zacharias, of the division of the course, and his wife was of the daughters of Aaron and her name was Elizabeth.

– LUKE 1: 5-6

The name Elizabeth means, "God is my oath," or "a worshiper of God." And the name Zacharias denotes, "Jehovah is renown."

Scripture tells us both of these individuals were *"righteous before God, walking in all the commandments and ordinances of the Lord blameless"* (Luke 1:6 KJV).

I like the last word, "blameless." This doesn't refer to just one, but both husband and wife. These two were chosen by God to become the father of John—the man who later baptized Jesus in the river Jordan.

The fact they were blameless before the Lord doesn't mean they never sinned. It refers to the fact that when God forgives, He forgets. We are restored to "right standing" before the Father.

In marriage, when you say or do something against your spouse, immediately bring the matter before the Lord and ask His pardon. You must also ask your mate to forgive you. The Word teaches that if we fail to forgive we cannot be forgiven.

This is important since if you can't find it in your heart to forgive your husband or wife, you are in trouble with God.

GREAT EXPECTATIONS

Despite your differences, do whatever it takes to stay on the same page.

There will probably be times your spouse wakes up in the morning with great expectations and wants you to help him or her accomplish a task that same day. If you are not singing the same song your partner doesn't have a clue about your thoughts and plans. So the objectives are not accomplished and your mate is upset because you were not able to read their mind.

Unfulfilled expectations are one of the greatest hurdles for couples to negotiate.

Talk it out. Learn in *advance* what will please your partner, then willingly do everything in your power to make it happen.

YOUR FORTRESS!

There may be moments in your marriage when an emptiness settles upon your partner's life that cannot be fulfilled by you. Some voids can only be replenished by God.

Don't be ashamed to admit your powerlessness in such a situation. What a wonderful time to pray together and tell the Lord how much you depend on Him.

Here is how David expressed the feelings of his heart:

*I will love you oh Lord, my strength. The Lord is
my rock and my fortress, and my deliverer; my God,
my strength, in whom I will trust; my shield and the
horn of my salvation, my stronghold.*

– PSALM 18:1-2

It is the Lord who is our deliverer!

Since your mate was not created to handle all of your problems, stop trying to make your spouse become your rock. In fact, trying to place all your expectations on your spouse only creates frustration and bewilderment.

CAN THEY COPE?

Too often we allow ourselves to associate with people and enter into a serious relationship without checking the person's ability to cope with major issues. Yes, we lean on the Lord, yet we need the strength of someone standing beside us during trying moments. As one woman said to her prospective husband, "Are you sure you can handle me?"

It's not that you are demanding or face weighty problems, but you must recognize what God has purposed for your future and decide whether He wants you to go any further in a relationship that could lead to marriage.

Because of what God has called you to do and has planned for your future, the person you choose as a spouse must be able to handle your assignment. If not, then you may be miserable for the rest of your days.

Remember, God's grace comes with every assignment He gives us. It's our obligation to make sure we are fulfilling a mission ordained by the Lord—and be certain our spouse's grace is meant for us, not someone else.

When you make a wrong choice, don't blame others. After all, it was you who made the bad decision.

Always allow your spirit to adjust to your spouse's grace and understand that your partner in life will never fulfill all your expectations. It will never happen!

No one can replace the power and purpose of the Lord.

HEARING FROM HEAVEN

Your home must be a stronghold for righteousness so others can sense God's presence when they enter your door. Visitors should be able to discern His glory continually dwelling and abiding. This requires a daily re-commitment from your spouse to be filled with the Spirit. Spend quality and quantity time necessary to hear from heaven. Only then will you be able to share what God is saying to you as a team.

Every couple must desire to see their home become a citadel for Christ.

WHOSE AGENDA?

Many enter into marriage, have children and slowly allow the pressures of life to consume and overwhelm them. They spend every waking hour watching over the safety of the kids, worrying about bills that need to be paid and figuring out what they need to do to advance their career.

Without realizing what has happened, the cares of the world, plus our own agendas, have pushed God out of the equation. Our priorities no longer allow Christ to reveal His Lordship over our household.

Your home serves a purpose established by God. Since He united you and your spouse for a divine reason, your focus should be on seeking the Lord's desires and His destiny.

Recognize what He wants to accomplish through your marriage and stay submitted to His will. As the psalmist writes:

> *Blessed is everyone who fears the Lord, who walks in His ways...*
> — PSALM 128:1

Men, you are a genuine leader in your family when you fear the Lord and have a true reverence for Him. The word "blessed" means *happy*—and that is what you will be when you act according to His Word.

The Lord also tells you, *"When you eat the labor of your hands, you shall be happy."* God will allow you to prosper if you honor and trust Him.

Even more, when you provide the right leadership your wife will produce, prosper and become fruitful in your home. The Bible says, *"Your wife shall be like a fruitful vine in the very heart of your house..."* *"Your children, like olive plants, all around your table."*

Because of the perpetual melody and rhythm flowing from you and your wife, the children will be able to follow your example of leadership.

An olive plant represents productivity, fruitfulness, substance and oil—very expensive items in Bible times. So God is saying He will make your children prosperous all around you.

CREATING THE ENVIRONMENT

By setting the spiritual tone and creating space for your wife to accomplish what is necessary, her creative juices will begin to flow and she will make your home to look like a palace.

You set the tone first, then the melody begins to play. The key is to be sure it's a Godly tone which fills your home every day—not a carnal jive or jazz.

Are you creating the environment which invites the Holy Spirit inside? This is what turns a house into a home.

Read the Gospels and you will find that Jesus never departed from the ways of His Father. Likewise, a man must be cautious of the spirits he allows to be released where he and his family resides.

DIFFERENT PATTERNS

It's not easy trying to cope with male-female temperaments, dispositions, thought patterns and how we think and respond to life. In many instances the male is optimistic while the female worries.

Man was created with the ability to be logical and he's always looking into the future, while the woman dwells in the present. She often asks, "How are we going to pay these bills? Where's the money coming from?"

The man assures her, "Look, don't worry about it. Everything's going to be just fine."

The wife may not fully understand what God has said to her husband. But if she has seen him operate in a godly manner, she will trust him and help him fulfill his role.

Man has an obligation to be the "life giver"—meaning he helps bring life to what God has given him. When he exhibits faith, his wife needs to join him in the vision.

Both partners must commit to discover and understand their mate's role and function, and develop a respect for it.

One of the greatest deterrents to a marriage is when partners fail to take time to discover their mate's role and function. It is vital to know what God has asked each to achieve in life and their place within the marriage.

When these questions have been identified and accepted, there will be an understanding between them that bathes their home with peace.

SHE IS "BLESSED"

The woman described in Proverbs 31 knew exactly what her life was about. The Bible says, *"Her husband is respected at the city gate, where he takes his seat among the elders of the land...She watches over the affairs of her household and does not eat the bread of idleness. Her children arise and call her blessed; her husband also, and he praises her"* Proverbs 31:23; 27-28 NIV).

Why is she so lauded by her husband? Because she had no problem fulfilling her role.

His assignment was to sit with the city fathers, while her's was to take care of the house. The reason she is not grumbling and complaining is because she knows her job and does it well.

When a husband and wife understand God's purpose is first and foremost, they will also understand the absolute necessity for their own existence.

It is only when we come to know our unique positions at home and in society that we are able to appreciate each other's function. Remember, the man is not independent of the woman, neither is the woman independent of the man in the Lord.

We need each other because God's purpose cannot be

fulfilled unless men and women are working together!

Men, get rid of your pride and lay aside that ego so you can understand how much you need a woman, and dear lady, you need that man!

BRIDGING THE GAP

Is Christ truly the Lord of your life? Is He the one in ultimate control? If not, you are inviting demonic forces into your home.

Remember, each time you stop playing your note, you make room for another note to be played. Lucifer is skilled in music; he can sing and accompany himself at the same time. The Bible says he has pipes in his body and can play music while singing.

Let me assure you Satan will introduce an evil song into your home. He comes disguised as an angel of light and can make his music sound sweet, melodious, and so appealing you think you need to hear more. Beware! Those sounds are nothing but noise!

If you are serious about resolving this infernal dispute, get in one accord with the Giver of Life and become like-minded.

The apostle Paul admonishes both parties to have the same love—one for the other. It is the only way the gap will be bridged and discord will be replaced with God's harmony.

CHAPTER SEVEN

POSITION AND AUTHORITY

Since the beginning of time, mankind has been intent on perverting what God established as the standards for life.

The Creator's initial desire was to duplicate heaven on earth. He decided to use a man and woman to accomplish His divine will for us to have dominion over all the earth according to Genesis 1:26. His attributes of holiness, purity, sanctity, sacredness, glory and honor were intended to be portrayed as our daily lifestyle—not the dictates of our flesh or societal standards.

History has shown that when God initiates a particular directive or mandate, man always seems to find ways of constructing laws contrary to His desires. It is obvious many are not content doing things God's way, rather, they allow themselves to be led by feelings and emotions. As a result they are literally at war with their Maker.

God knew what His plans were before He created man in His image. Man, however, even after hearing the grand design and knowing the greatness of the Father, still chose to disobey.

Such an attitude prevails today—even among some who confess and profess Christ as their Lord and Savior.

OUR STUBBORN WILL

Somehow, millions have grown comfortable compromising God's standards. After being given the choice, they decide not to live holy and pure before the Father. Often there is virtually no consideration for what the Lord has given us or what He has done in our lives.

Man's stubborn will and humanistic perceptions have produced devastating circumstances in the nations of our world.

How we look at things or view life, shapes us into who we become.

What we perceive is based on education, environment and experience. Our world view is the result of where we have been, how we were raised and what we have learned and witnessed. These determine how we respond to a given situation.

The result of these factors cause many to function

totally out of the will of God. Instead we choose man-made decisions rather than those pleasing to the Father. In the process we fail to hear God's voice and miss His directives.

When we operate in our own will, it can produce tragic consequences—the result of operating on assumptions which are often false. We make major mistakes and base our lives on those errors

The recurring and subsequent events are no longer the devil's responsibility, but a matter of exercising our own will. An outside force didn't cause our problem. We made a conscious decision to close our ears to the Lord and exercise an attitude that allows us to become rebellious, obstinate and disobedient.

Don't blame the devil because he has nothing to do with it. You exercised your own will and perception.

INSTANT JUDGMENTS

Inward thinking eventually has an outward manifestation. For example, we treat people according to how we think about them. We look at others with perceived views based on our thoughts concerning them. We're not looking at who they really are spiritually, but what they present to us outwardly.

It is human nature to make instant judgments of others which aren't true since we didn't take the time to get to know the individual. Only later do we realize we have misunderstood motives and behaviors. Why do we allow ourselves to form quick conclusions or opinions before we have taken the time to understand their circumstances?

"MADE IN HEAVEN"

Unfortunately, by relying on self rather than God, we can make the most tragic mistake of all—choosing the wrong mate for our lifelong companion. The Bible is filled with divine directives and words of wisdom which truly can produce a marriage "made in heaven."

When you shared your marital vows, you made a covenant to respect your spouse. That was not a conditional vow. God stipulated from the beginning man and woman were equal—and they should mutually share authority on the earth.

Man is not the authority and woman is not the authority. They *share* the authority.

I can hear some Bible student saying, "But wait a minute! Didn't God curse them in the garden?"

Yes, He did. He cursed both the man and the woman. But, upon receiving Jesus as Savior and Lord, the curse is reversed, and we go back to the original state before the fall. What is that?

And God blessed them, and God
told them to have dominion.
– GENESIS 1:28

God said man and woman are supposed to reign on the earth and have authority co-equally. This is supposed to be the status both husband and wife share in a marital relationship. No one is above another. We are equal in essence, but different in function.

The reason we have been given separate roles to fill is to make sure we accomplish God's mandate to dominate the earth. He desires to have a husband and wife working collaboratively and corporately in accomplishing His Will. In doing so, we complete God's plan and no one becomes inferior.

A PRE-ORDAINED POSITION

Just because God told the woman to be submissive does not make her subordinate; and because the Creator instructed the man to lead, does not make him superior. It is mutual respect which is designed to exist between a husband and wife at all times.

A man has no right to tell a woman, "Step back to your position."

The wife has as much authority as a man, and the only reason he has been given the leadership position is because of God's grace. Someone has to make a final decision and God designated the man for the role.

Remember, the Creator started with the male and placed everything He wanted to accomplish in him *first*. The only reason a man has been assigned to lead is because of his pre-ordained position. He is the foundation of the family and should be honored as such.

If you owe someone honor or respect, "Pay up!" The Bible makes this clear:

> *Give everyone what you owe him. If you owe*
> *taxes, pay taxes; if revenue, then revenue; if respect,*
> *then respect; if honor, then honor.*
> — ROMANS 13-7 NIV

TOTAL EQUALITY

Spiritually, there is total equality between a man and a woman. God's Word tells us:

> *There is neither Jew nor Greek, there is neither slave*
> *nor free, there is neither male nor female, for you are all one*
> *in Christ Jesus. And if you are Christ's, then you are*
> *Abraham's seed, and heirs according to the promise.*
> — GALATIANS 3:28-29

This is made clear when an individual receives an inheritance. A man does not get any more from the estate because he is a male and a woman does not receive a larger share because she is a female. Both are equal before the courts.

It is also true in heaven's economy. Since we are all equal in Christ, we are "heirs according to the promise."

We are spirit beings and a spirit has no gender. Man is what God made. Think of it this way: God is spirit, and because He is, man is spirit also. There's a spirit of man in the female, and a spirit of man in the male.

> *Let us make man in Our image,*
> *according to Our likeness...*
> — GENESIS 1:26

KEEPING SCORE

Regardless of our equality, personal experiences can cause people to openly disrespect each other.

In the game of life, however, God does not want us to tally wrongs committed nor keep a scorecard on how many times we strike out.

More often than not, we do not readily dismiss the offenses of others. Instead, we allow subsequent actions to build up in our mind until it reaches a point we don't know how to deal with the person or issue. The resentment runs deep. However, scripture says:

> *Great peace have they that love your*
> *law and nothing shall offend them.*
> — PSALMS 119:165

When we feel wronged and our spirit becomes wounded there is a "retaliation spirit" in us which surfaces and says, "I'm determined in some way or another to get back at you. I will do it even at the point of being silent. I will hurt you the way you've dishonored me."

THE TRUE YOU

In marriage, without thinking, the sword called our tongue can inflict lasting wounds. It can reach the place where we dishonor our mate without any regard for their feelings. Then, instead of repenting, we find a justification for our behavior.

One husband told his wife, "Look I'm sorry I hurt you, but I meant what I said."

Is that an apology? Remember:

Out of the abundance of the heart the mouth speaks.
— MATTHEW 12:34

If you make a statement which pierces the spirit of another, I believe you *intended* to wound the person. Sadly, we may develop the habit of speaking before our mind has time to catch up with our mouth. If we would just take a "time out" to consider our words before uttering them, perhaps we would avoid the damage we inflict.

Some people are "sharp tongued" yet are subtle in the way they wound others with words. What they say may be spoken softly, yet with a piercing, caustic attitude.

A BRUISED EGO

In the book of Esther, a king by the name of Ahasuerus was no different. According to scripture, he had little consideration for his wife:

*On the seventh day when the heart of the king was
merry with wine, he commanded Mehuman, Biztha,
Harbona, Bigtha, Abagtha, Zethar, and Carcas seven eunuchs
who served in the presence of king Ahasuerus,
to bring queen Vashti before the king, wearing her royal
crown, in order to show her beauty, in order to show her
beauty to the people and the officials, for she was beautiful
to behold. But queen Vashti refused to come at the king's
command, brought by his eunuchs, therefore the king
was furious and his anger burned within him.*

— ESTHER 1:10-12

The only reason this King Ahasuerus called for his queen was to show her off. She was nothing more than a showpiece, a trophy wife.

Men must understand that women are not just an object of affection, but breathing, living human beings who deserve every right they are entitled to receive.

The King was really saying, *"Look, just stand there and let them look at you."* But he had no consideration for his wife because the Bible records, *"He commanded those men,"* and they had to go and get her. "The king said he wants you now," and Vashti refused.

She disobeyed because the law of the Medes and Persians stated that the queen had access to the king only once every thirty days. She could not come into his presence at any other time.

Furthermore, Vashti could only enter if he extended his scepter. If not, she could possibly die. So she refused;

131

because the law stated that a woman was never supposed to come into the presence of men while they were drinking or drunk also.

Vashti understood protocol, and she refused to do anything outside the law. Therefore, she was well within her right not to show up.

King Ashuerus became angry because Vashti was defiant in the company of his men. His ego was bruised and he became quite disrespectful.

According to scripture we read:

> *Be kindly affectionate to one another with brotherly love in honor giving preference to one another.*
> — ROMANS 12:10

We should always look for ways to exalt our spouse and prefer them to ourselves. It is important to understand why our mate has responded negatively over a particular matter. In this case, the king's men were ranked higher than his wife and had greater access to him than the queen.

There are certain instances when we don't want to be approached by our spouse—or anyone else. We prefer to be in our own world and our own space. Then, when our territory is invaded, we see it as a sign of disrespect.

You storm off in a huff, yet in your marriage covenant you vowed you wanted to be with your mate for the rest of your life.

THE "SNOWBALL EFFECT"

Back to our story. The King asked:

> *What shall we do to queen Vashti, according to*
> *law, because she did not obey the command of king*
> *Ahasuerus brought to her by the eunuchs?*
> — ESTHER 1:15

Remember, this is her husband asking a group of men (political officials) what he should do with *his* wife. He obviously has no respect for her.

When we are equal partners we are equal in authority. The greatest fear most spouses experience is that once the spirit of disrespect has been allowed to enter, it may have a "snowball effect." So we become guarded and live defensively. As a result, communication is strained.

Important issues can go un-addressed because couples are afraid of the aftermath. That's what happened in this biblical account:

> *And Memucan answered before the king and the*
> *princes, queen Vashti has not only wronged the king,*
> *but also all the princes and all the people who are in*
> *all the provinces of king Ahasuerus. For the queen's*
> *behavior will become known to all women.*
> — ESTHER 1:16

Here's the snowball:

133

*So they will despise their husbands in their eyes
when they report king Ahasuerus commanded queen Vashti
to be brought in before him, but she did not come. This very
day the noble ladies of Persia and Media will say to all the
king's officials that they have heard of the behavior of the
queen, thus there will be excessive contempt and wrath.*
−ESTHER 1:17

There was an explosion of disdain toward the king.

WHAT BRINGS DISHONOR?

There are numerous doors through which dishonor
can enter a marriage. Here are ten key factors:

1. Ignoring or degrading another person's opinions, advice, or beliefs.

What was your response when your spouse gave you
an opinion or advice concerning a matter which involves
you both? Did you give him or her the courtesy of an
answer or respond with a blank stare?

It's possible to look at another person without
listening—nothing registering at all. When this happens
it is a form of total disrespect. It is also dishonoring since
you are communicating, "You really don't have anything
to tell me."

Just as troublesome is when you give the response,
"That's stupid!" Or, "How dumb! Why in the world
would you say that?"

134

Again, unnecessary disrespect.

2. Burying yourself in the television or newspaper when another person is trying to communicate with you.

Your spouse is trying to converse with you about something that's important, yet you remain glued to the TV, watching the news or continue reading the sports section of the daily paper. There's absolutely no eye contact.

To you the communication may seem insignificant and unimportant, yet it may loom as a much larger matter to the one asking the question.

Do you and your mate both a favor by paying attention when spoken to.

3. Creating jokes concerning another person's weaknesses or shortcomings.

Avoid comments such as, "Can't you do anything with your hair? It looks like a tornado just blew through the house."

Or, you are having dinner with your family at a fast food restaurant and comment about your son, "Have you noticed Johnny's ears lately? Look how big they are!"

This is not only rude, but can cause Johnny to be insecure and chip away at his self-esteem. After the laughter fades, there may be long-lasting wounds.

4. *Making regular verbal attacks on loved ones and criticizing them harshly, being judgmental, or delivering uncaring lectures.*

It's dangerous when one person thinks they know the Bible so well they are always telling others "what the Lord says." I've even known wives who "minister" to their husbands by preaching a little sermon at the breakfast table. In truth, the are "venting" what they would like to see changed in their mate—under the guise of letting "God" do the talking.

Even worse is the person who starts blasting a friend concerning something they don't like about him or her.

5. *Treating in-laws or other relatives as unimportant in planning and communication.*

A husband or wife may not want to have anything to do with the parents or relatives of the spouse. They find any excuse to stay away from an activity that involves these people.

To disrespect your in-laws or any relative is a sign of immaturity.

The Word counsels we are to live "peaceably" with others. Take the high road and welcome your extended family.

6. *Ignoring or simply not expressing appreciation for kind deeds.*

If you truly honor and respect your partner, you'll acknowledge even the smallest favor. Don't wait until he or she goes "beyond the call of duty" to say thanks.

After all, if the person you love takes the time to think about you, why remain silent? The best way to show kindness is with kindness.

7. Distasteful habits that are displayed in front of the family.

When a member of your family comes to the dinner table chewing gum with an open mouth, don't hesitate to have a little conversation. If it continues, the person is showing disrespect and there are larger issues involved.

A periodic discussion of proper etiquette, courtesy and manners is always worth the time and effort.

8. Over committing ourselves to projects or people.

Balance your time to include your spouse.

If, because of the pressures of life, you begin to spend more hours outside the home than in, something is out of kilter. This is especially true if the activities don't include your mate.

In time, your partner will begin to rebel—because he or she feels those interests are more important to you. Perhaps it's time to take a fresh look at your schedule.

9. Power struggles which leave a person feeling dominated.

I've counseled those who live in fear because of the

verbal and emotional abuse hurled at them by their mate. If left unchecked and ignored, it may lead to physical abuse.

In most instances, men are predominantly responsible for these power struggles which turn violent—psychologically or otherwise. Although it is usually a sign of a weak man seeking to exert his control, the woman may live in fear and terror. Her "macho" man is really a coward and serious counseling is needed.

10. Unwillingness to admit wrongdoing or ask for forgiveness.

I'm sure you have encountered men or women so filed with pride they simply cannot bring themselves to the place where they admit, "I was wrong!"

Even after some people are *proven* to be in error, they still won't ask for forgiveness. Instead, they mutter, "Well, that's your opinion," or "If that's what you believe, that's okay. We just won't talk about it anymore."

When this happens between spouses, it's time to communicate until there is a resolution.

IT'S MUTUAL

Respect and honor should be mutual—and it cannot be forced. It is also reciprocal. In the words of Jesus:

Therefore whatever you want men to do to you, do also to them, for this is the law and the prophets.
– MATTHEW 7:12

"The Golden Rule" applies to every aspect of life. When you esteem others, you will be esteemed.

Respect is earned. You can't demand it.

I love the sound advice given by the apostle Peter: *"Finally, all of you, live in harmony with one another; be sympathetic, love as brothers, be compassionate and humble. Do not repay evil with evil or insult with insult, but with blessing, because to this you were called so that you may inherit a blessing"* (1 Peter 8-9) NIV).

In a mutual relationship, a person does not try to overpower his or her mate. Both parties must understand they have equal authority. In the words of the apostle Paul:

Therefore as the elect of God, holy and beloved, put on tender mercies, kindness, humility, meekness, longsuffering, bearing with one another, and forgiving one another. If anyone has a complaint against another, even as Christ forgave you, so you also must do. But above all these things, put on love, which is the bond, or the glue of perfection.
– COLOSSIANS 3:12-14

If you are guilty of any form of disrespect, resolve the dispute with humility and ask forgiveness. Love and appreciation must be practiced and demonstrated every day. Instead of dishonoring, start encouraging. Instead of criticizing, start congratulating!

Perhaps it's your spouse who has the problem of dishonoring. If that's the case, continue to do what you know is right in the eyes of God. Then pray your mate will have a changed heart and a new attitude.

Often the things we consider disrespectful are really misunderstandings—and we are admonished in the Word to be slow in becoming angry. Always give your partner the benefit of the doubt.

Kindness is received when kindness is offered! Love is received when love is given.

Agape love is the glue of perfection.

Regardless of the situation in the marriage, strive to reach out to your spouse with a pure heart and seek godly counsel.

Remember, the enemy wants to divide God's church and we must prove him to be what he is—a liar.

None of us are perfect but we have the Holy Spirit who is our Helper and will lead and guide us into all truth.

CHAPTER EIGHT

CHOICES

No airplane pilot worth his wings leaves the ground without a flight plan. The choices he makes on the path to the final destination will always be guided by purpose. As bestselling author, Dr. Myles Munroe says: *"Like a pilot's flight plan, purpose also serves as a guide for determining the best path to a predetermined end."*

This same principle applies to the choice we make in selecting our partner for life—our destination in marriage. What is the outcome when the mate you chose is not the mate you need?

God created us with specific needs that are pertinent and intertwined with our specific assignment here on earth. Certain elements required for me to live a quality life are not going to be the same as yours, because you were created differently for a unique purpose.

No two people are the same. There will be times your needs may be greater than mine, and mine greater than yours.

"Purpose serves as a guide for determining the best path to a predetermined end."
– DR. MYLES MUNROE

Every person desires to be fulfilled—and no one wants to live a life of *void* or feel a sense of emptiness. To counteract being lonely, we involve ourselves in a variety of projects, believing as long as there is some sort of continuous activity in our existence we are being fulfilled.

However, even with this "busyness," the void remains and we search for an answer for personal satisfaction and a "meaning" to our lives. Often we will look at those around us and discover we aren't in the right relationship. Desperate, we pray, "Lord, I know you have given me a unique design and assignment on this earth and I am committed to achieving it. But please, God, send the right person to help me."

There are no adequate words to describe the feeling of being *unfulfilled.*

BACK TO SQUARE ONE

As we journey through life and discover the needs to be met and satisfied, we realize we can't provide all the answers by ourselves. So we reach out and begin to interact with others—part of the human experience.

Here's the problem. While trying to satisfy our own

desires, we may connect and attach ourselves to a person who does not have the same requirements we have. Consequently, we end up back at square one, feeling isolated and alone.

What's our next course of action? To find someone else to fulfill what we are searching for. This is the reason many people change partners consistently. In their search, some will decide to get married—believing the old adage, "Something is better than nothing."

Pay heed to God's warning:

There is a way that seems right unto a man, but the end thereof, is the ways of death.
– PROVERBS 14:12

Each time we enter a new relationship we seek fresh ways to respond to that individual. We rationalize and say, "Well, this seems right" — not realizing the possible dangerous consequences.

In this process, we fail to understand that *no* earthly person will ever be able to meet all of our deepest needs. As we continue, this will become abundantly clear.

UNREALISTIC THINKING

The reason we are not able to find answers outside ourselves is because the solution lies within *us*. However, this fact is far from our minds as we run faster, and with more desperation, seeking either material possessions or one more person we feel will bridge the gap and fill the emptiness.

Not only is it unrealistic to think we can find our life in someone else, it is unfair to place such pressure on another individual.

We must discover *who we are* before we stand before God and exchange our marital vows.

> *Thus says the Lord, cursed is the man who trusts in man and makes flesh his strength, whose heart departs from the Lord.*
> — JEREMIAH 17:5

Rather than depending on God to meet your needs, you look for them to be met through your spouse. According to this scripture, the Lord says you have invited a "curse."

We must never allow anyone other than Almighty God to become our strength.

MORE THAN "I LOVE YOU"

If you are single, I suggest you and your future life partner discuss your expectations—so you can determine whether each of you has the grace to meet one another's needs.

Just because a person says "I love you," does not mean that he or she has all it takes to cope with your purpose and destiny.

If you really understand the assignment for which you have been created, you should not marry anyone who does not fit the description God has for your life. Don't allow your emotions to turn your attention to outward beauty, or even the other person's career. Find out whether your desired partner has the grace to meet your needs in the long term.

As you grow older, your requirements and focus may change. That's why there must be an open discussion about each person's desires. To blindly live with the notion "love covers all" is a mistake and a lie. Love may cover a multitude of sin, but it does not cover *all*.

WHAT'S IN THE BOX?

Be warned! Like a wedding present, you can marry an individual and think you have received the ultimate gift until the "wrappings" are removed. When you untie the bow and tear off the pretty paper, there is nothing left except an empty cardboard box. Appearances can be deceiving. If we fail to grasp our needs are spiritual, we run the risk of placing unnecessary burdens on our mate. Since there are issues that can only be handled by the Almighty, pray for the wisdom of the Holy Spirit to give you the discernment to know the difference between a natural need and one that is spiritual.

Many remain on a merry-go-round for years thinking all their problems are earth based and in the natural. The barrier to the solution, however, may be because they don't have the right relationship with God.

People often enter into marriage and, in the elation of their "honeymoon" period, spend less and less time in the presence of the Lord. They no longer read the Word and, as a result, fail to converse with their mate about spiritual matters.

Eventually, since the God-factor is absent in their relationship, they believe the only way they can fulfill themselves is with each other. Before long they become extremely possessive, not wanting the other person out of their sight. When an earthly person is all we have to hold and rely on, it is frightening indeed!

King David understood this. He did not place his faith in man's strength or abilities to meet his needs. Instead, he looked to the Almighty. As he expressed it:

Some trust in chariots, and some in horses, but we will remember the name of the Lord our God.
– PSALM 20:7

THE "BETROTHAL"

In Old Testament times, a woman had little choice regarding who would become her husband because marriage took place through a *betrothal* system. Two men would get together and make a covenant with one another. If one man had a daughter and another had a son, they would vow, "When my daughter is of age, she will be the wife of your son."

Because of this covenant, boys and girls had no input in their own fate. They *would* one day be married.

In some instances, the two men would seal the oath by cutting a bull in half and placing the two pieces side by side. As the blood flowed on the ground they would walk between the two halves and make their covenant. In essence, it was at that point the marriage took place—even though it would be many years later before the actual ceremony occurred and the couple began living together as husband and wife.

Here is an example of a pre-arranged marriage from the book of 1 Samuel:

Now when Abigail saw David, she dismounted quickly from the donkey, fell on her face before David, and bowed down to the ground. So she fell at his feet and said, On me, my lord, on me let this iniquity be! And please let your maidservant speak in your ears, and hear the words of your maidservant. Please, let not my lord regard this scoundrel Nabal. For as his name is, so is he. Nabal is his name, and folly is with him. But I, your maidservant, did not see the young men of my lord whom you sent.

– 1 SAMUEL 25:23-25

Now therefore, my lord, as the Lord lives, and as your soul lives, since the Lord has held you back from coming to bloodshed and from avenging yourself with your own hand, now then, let your enemies and those who seek harm for my lord be as Nabal. And now this present that your maidservant has brought to my lord, let it be given to the young men who follow my lord. "Please forgive the trespass of your maidservant. For the Lord will certainly make for my lord an enduring house, because my lord fights the battles of the Lord and evil is not found in you throughout your days.

– 1 SAMUEL 25:26-28

Abigail's father informed her she would be marrying someone given to "folly" because Nabal's name literally means "a fool." Imagine the fear which gripped Abigail's heart regarding her impending marriage to a man who was known by such a name.

There are many such Abigails in the world today. A woman who knows the groom she is marrying is a fool, yet marries him anyway, reveals desperation in her own life. Often she is aware he has no direction or purpose — and is completely frivolous and unwise. Yet, she forges ahead.

Abigail, it seems, had no choice. She was being forced to enter into a marriage with a man who had shown himself to be irresponsible.

SECRETS WILL BE REVEALED

People seldom reveal their negative side in the beginning of a relationship. Then, as the years unfold, little by little the unbecoming traits in the other individual's life begin to surface.

Don't ignore this warning:

> *For there is nothing hidden which will not*
> *be revealed, nor has anything been kept secret*
> *but that it should come to light.*
> *— MARK 4:22*

Marrying the wrong person can cause you to carry a burden, that unless the Lord intervenes, you don't have the strength to bear. Suppose a woman marries a man because she's looking for a leader, but later discovers *he* needs to be led. Likewise, a man marries a woman whom he thinks is going to be a helper, and then learns she's a hindrance.

Too late, he finds she is not able to give input into helping him make decisions or provide support in the home and with the family. As a result, he is left to run the household.

DON'T BLAME THE FOOL!

In the story of Abigail, she realized the error of her husband's ways:

> *Now when Abigail saw David, she dismounted quickly from the donkey, fell on her face before David and bowed down to the ground.*
>
> – 1 SAMUEL 25:23

Abigail did this because David, through his servants, had sent for Nabal, asking him for some food. At the time, David was watching over Nabal's flocks along with the man's servants.

Nabal, being the fool he was, said, "No, I'm not giving David anything. It doesn't impress me he is supposed to be the next king. That doesn't matter to me at all."

The servant quickly ran and told Abigail who realized what was happening. Knowing full well he was saying this to the future ruler of Israel, she jumped on her donkey and went to see David. Scripture records how she fell at his feet and asked him not to listen to this "scoundrel" Nabal. That was a strong statement, especially since she was talking about her husband.

Abigail said, "Don't blame Nabal, blame me!"

THE HEAVY BURDEN

The law of Christ is for us to love one another, even as Christ has loved us. This is the fulfillment of the law. As the apostle Paul writes, we are to love that individual and take on the weight of their burden—even when we don't want to.

> *Bear one another's burdens*
> *and so fulfill the law of Christ.*
> – GALATIANS 6:2

I have counseled those who want to end a marriage because their spouse has become emotionally detached and they complain, "My needs are not being fulfilled." In other cases, one partner complains, "They have a controlling spirit."

One man told me, "She takes over and acts like the man of the house. Every opinion or suggestion I make is discarded." He confided he didn't even want to make love anymore because, "I don't like to make love to a another man!"

Unfortunately, there are some men who actually *look* for a woman who can dominate them. These individuals usually have a docile, passive spirit, and need another to lead them.

OH, WHAT LOVE DOES!

If you want the best advice on love, turn to the first letter Paul wrote to the believers at Corinth. He begins by saying, *"Love suffers long"* (1 Corinthians 13:4). This means it is supposed to give you the ability to put up with *anything*—even when your mate is not meeting your needs. You don't detach yourself emotionally just because your partner has shortcomings.

Paul continues, *"Love does not envy, love does not parade itself, love is not puffed up, does not behave rudely, does not seek it's own, is not provoked, thinks no evil, does not rejoice in iniquity but rejoices in the truth"* (vv.5-6).

What else does love do? *"Love bears all things, believes all things"*

True love believes that one day things are going to get better. There may be many sleepless nights, but the deep affection God places in your heart endures *all things*. It gives hope and never dissipates or fades.

Are you willing to go through the trials and tough times? Remember, the Word tells us, *"Love never fails, but whether there are prophecies they will fail, whether there are tongues they will cease, whether there is knowledge, it will vanish away, but love never fails"* (v.8).

When needs are not being met we may begin to see our mate as our *project*, as opposed to being our husband or wife. "I'm working on him," says one wife. Or, "I am trying to get her straightened out," comments a husband.

When this happens, our responses to our partner aren't being appropriately shown. You look at your spouse as an individual you've been assigned to—as a project to "fix" or a mission to "mend."

As a result, some marriages become nothing more than a business relationship. In these cases, couples may relate to each other only with surface-level conversation, failing to talk about what truly matters. They don't discuss love or speak of the intimacies a husband and wife would normally verbalize. Rarely does the talk center on their relationship.

Abigail, in calling Nabal a "scoundrel," obviously viewed him as a project. No doubt, however, every human being is a work in progress.

BACK TO BASICS

If primary human needs are not being met, what is left for a person to do? That's the question asked by the psalmist:

If the foundations are destroyed,
what can the righteous do?
— PSALM 11:3

Perhaps we should look at the basics. How in this world can we see the real problem when we never take the time to establish a foundation? Foolishly, we try to build a house on *nothing.*

And except the Lord build the
house, they labor in vain that build it.
— PSALM 127:1

Make a commitment to place God first in your life and make Him the center of your marriage. Only then will your priorities be in the right place.

The next step involves recognizing the three spirits which are manifest when you feel trapped and miserable in you relationship:

1. Misery leads to *anger.*
2. Anger leads to *resentment.*
3. Resentment leads to *fear.*

You grow angry because you realize you moved too impulsively, and then become upset with your mate for not meeting your needs. You feel, "I could have done better," so you resent your partner for being oblivious to your basic desires.

When this happens it's time to turn to God's Word:

Let all bitterness, wrath anger, clamor, and evil speaking be put away from you with all malice, and be kind to one another, tender hearted, forgiving one another, just as God in Christ forgave you.
— EPHESIANS 4:31-32

God will pardon you for deviating from His eternal plan. By receiving someone into your life He did not approve of, you stepped out of His *perfect* will to option for His *permissive* will. You were moved by your flesh and not by the Spirit—and received what you wanted rather than what you needed.

THE "FANTASYLAND"

Many struggle through life holding onto unreasonable expectations, living in the world of "what should be" rather than   reality. In other words, they exist in a fantasyland, always pretending everything is fine. It's time to step out of that make-believe existence and understand you are in the real world.

Fantasy consumes reality when our quest is for "the perfect mate." We will die without discovering such an individual because no flawless man or woman exists on this planet. The only perfect Man who ever lived is seated on the right hand of our Father in heaven.

Remember, God is still working on you—you're still under construction!

For we know in part, and we prophesy in part,
but when that which is perfect is come, then that
which is in part shall be done away.
– 1 CORINTHIANS 13:9-10

The reason we only know "in part" is because the life of Christ has yet to be fully manifested in us.

To put it another way, we have "a part," others have "a part" and Christ has "a part." Together, we are to make the melody and harmony to which we earlier referred.

"RESCUE ME!"

Pray for the individual God sends into your life.

When we resort to anger, we lose our willingness to forgive others. This often happens when our expectations and hopes fall flat.

We must not judge our mate unnecessarily when they do not live up to our dreams. Instead, pray the prayer of Abigail:

And it shall come to pass when the Lord has done for my lord according to all the good that He has spoken concerning you, and has appointed you ruler over Israel, that this will be no grief to you, nor offensive heart to my lord, even that you have shed blood without cause, or that my lord has avenged himself. But when the Lord has dealt with my lord, then remember your handmaid.
— SAMUEL 25:30-31

She was saying, "When you become king, make me your queen. Remember what I did for you, then come and rescue me."

ETERNAL LOVE

The only guarantee we have in this life is God's undying love for us, His children. It also applies to our interpersonal relationships. This is why God says:

I have loved you with an everlasting love, and with loving kindness have I drawn you.
— JEREMIAH 31-3

His love is eternal—it will *never* die.

Every level of existence is affected by the principles

you've been reading. You don't need an Abigail-Nabal relationship, because it is obvious their future was based on a crumbling foundation. No wonder Abigail said, "When you become king, please remember me."

Don't allow your partnership to enter into the cycle of misery, anger, resentment, or fear. Remember, when you opt for "things," people or activities in order to be fulfilled, there will always be bitter disappointment.

Let's face it: the truth about ourselves really hurts, so be honest concerning issues which need to be dealt with. Just because another individual has not met your hopes and longings does not mean they should be discarded. You still need to hold them near and dear while believing there is a heavenly purpose for your relationship.

When the Kingdom comes in both of you, situations which seemed to be insurmountable no longer loom as large as they once did. Even if there are felt needs which are *never* fulfilled, we must still praise God for those that are!

Satan's job is to *steal* marriages, *kill* relationships and *destroy* families. Be aware of his cunning devices and determine in your heart you are more than a conqueror through Christ Jesus.

Be sober, be vigilant; because your adversary the devil walks about like a roaring lion, seeking whom he may devour.
– 1 PETER 5:8

A PRAYER WORTH PRAYING
After reading these pages, if you feel your life with

your mate can be improved, then I urge you to repeat this prayer.

Heavenly Father, the word I have received has been mind-transforming, life-changing and correctional. Father, it has challenged me to take a deeper look at my relationships and, most of all, my unfulfilled needs, expectations, hopes, dreams and desires.

Father, I repent for placing undue desire and aspirations on my mate. I also repent, Lord, because I have not been honest about issues from my past life that were never dealt with and have blamed my mate for not filling those needs.

I am sorry, Heavenly Father, for being unforgiving, for allowing the spirits of anger, resentment and fear to creep into my life. I am sorry for allowing other things, people, and activities to fill a void, when the reality was I needed You. Forgive me for living in a fantasy world and teach me how to live in the world of reality. Help me to accept what is true and no longer live in an illusion of make-believe.

Father, show me those needs that are human or natural, and then reveal what can only be fulfilled in the Spirit realm. Help me to bring revival and restoration to our relationship; to see our home become holy ground once again; a place where we abound and abide in You.

I pray I will stop looking at my mate as a project; instead, as a loving human being created by You.
In Jesus Name, Amen.

I pray this book will bring positive changes in the lives of those who read it. May we begin to see relationships revived across this nation and around the world. We give You all the praise and honor and glory O God!

Thank you for allowing me to share my heart with you. I truly believe you can say farewell to the unresolved dispute and say hello to the most wonderful marriage ever. With God's help, there is marvelous hope and promise for your future.

FOR A COMPLETE LIST OF BOOKS
AND OTHER RESOURCES, OR TO SCHEDULE
THE AUTHOR FOR SPEAKING ENGAGEMENTS,
CONTACT:

BISHOP GILBERT COLEMAN, JR.
FREEDOM CHRISTIAN BIBLE FELLOWSHIP
6100 WEST COLUMBIA AVENUE
PHILADELPHIA, PA 19151

PHONE: 215-477-0800
FAX: 215-473-1640
TOLL FREE: 800-822-6335
EMAIL: FCBFChurch@aol.com
INTERNET: www.freedomworldwide.net